THE BLACK WIDOW

A Play in 9 Acts

By Charles Bennett

THE
BLACK
WIDOW

a play by
Charles Bennett

The Black Widow

© 2019 Charles Bennett

ISBN: 978-0-578-51898-5

For performance rights
and other permissions,
contact xavier_bennett69@yahoo.com

ACT 1 and 9 SETTING: Unfurnished

The play takes begins and ends in the present in Cleveland, Ohio. The Phat Kat is a bar and spoken word performance space. STAGE LEFT are a single café table and two café chairs. CENTER STAGE is a raised platform. Behind that is the entrance to the Phat Kat. STAGE RIGHT is a high bar table; behind that an empty bar shelf and a doorway leading into an office.

ACT 2-8 SETTING: Furnished

The same bar as it appeared one year before, decorated and lit for drinking and poetry. STAGE LEFT are facing couches. CENTER STAGE is the raised platform with stage lighting and a microphone stand. Behind is the doorway entrance into the Phat Kat lounge. STAGE RIGHT are a single café table and two café chairs, a high bar table and three high bar chairs; behind it a bar shelf filled with liquor bottles and a doorway leading into an office.

CHARACTERS

PROPERTY MANAGER	Small businessman, manages property for owner, late forties-fifties.
ZANE	A local neighborhood hustler. Early twenties.
LUCIANO	Co-owner of the Phat Kat lounge. Early thirties.
JOSHUA	Co-owner of the Phat Kat lounge and the host for poetry night. Late twenties.
LILY	A native of Louisiana who practices black magic. Mid-twenties.
ROSE	A native of Atlanta and an elementary school teacher. Mid-twenties.
JASMINE	A resident of the neighborhood and friends with Lily. Early thirties.
TERRANCE	A local poet. Early twenties.
REGGIE	A local poet and substitute teacher. Late twenties.
TIFFANY	An employee at the Phat Kat lounge. Early twenties.
HONEY	An inspiring poetry and music artist from the area. Early twenties.

ACT 1
SCENE 1

(Lights up on an unfurnished bar, with a performance stage.
ZANE unlocks the door and turns on only a few lights. The
PROPERTY MANAGER stands by the door, observing but
not seen by ZANE. ZANE gets on stage, clears his throat,
and gestures to an imaginary crowd)

ZANE:

If only I had the power to exemplify the joy you bring to me,

I would write a song so that birds could wake you
every morning to sing

beautiful tunes for you and our precious little baby.

In the oceans I would have all the dolphins unite,

form together to create a portrait of your lovely face,

and even in space and the angels in heaven could see

the love I have for you would spread across
this world's seven seas.

That's how much you mean to me.

I wish I could with a motion of my hand clear the skies,

so I could write this

poem so everyone could see with their eyes.

The sky would be my paper

THE BLACK WIDOW by Charles Bennett

and the clouds would be my ink.

So you could lift your head, read my words
and be tickled pink.

But for now I can't reach for the stars,

so baby please settle for

this little ass bar.

ZANE:

Man Josh would have tripped if he heard this.

PROPERTY MANAGER:

Umm, excuse me sir. This place is closed down for business

ZANE:

Oh, it's OK. I'm the new owner. Zane Phillips, and you are?

PROPERTY MANAGER:

(Startled and hesitates)

Oh, I'm the property manager. I come by and check on the place.
Make sure there isn't any suspect activity going on. So you are the
new owner. I heard you reading a poem. I heard this place was once a
poetry spot.

ZANE:

Yeah, I actually use to read here. I bought this place for my wife and
I. I plan on making it an open mic comedy spot, but when Josh was
here… (looking around) Yeah it was poetry.

PROPERTY MANAGER:

I heard you say Josh. Did you know Joshua?

ZANE:

Yeah, he was a very good friend of mine.

PROPERTY MANAGER:

They say that this place is haunted by his ghost, I heard so many
stories about him and...

(ZANE, very hostile, cuts him off)

ZANE:

And they were lies. First off he wasn't crazy; he became a victim of
lies, gossip, and jealousy.

PROPERTY MANAGER:

I didn't mean to get you upset Mr. Phillips. I was just curious to know
the whole story of this Josh guy. The previous owner was happy to
sell this place. He said it became a burden plus what had happened
with Josh.

ZANE:

Oh he was happy to sell it. He was all about that money. Because of Josh, I was able to get back with my girl and become a comedian. I bought this place because of all the love that took place here. I loved coming here and so did everybody else. Josh was the best friend I ever had and I truly miss him.

PROPERTY MANAGER:

Well look here man, I have nothing but time on my hands. Can you tell me the true story of Joshua, I would love to hear your side.

ZANE:

Yeah, my wife and my daughter aren't suppose to be here until later this evening. So if you want to hear a long story, I'm willing to tell it.

PROPERTY MANAGER:

Like I said, I have nothing but time on my hands. I am very patient.

ZANE:

I wish we all had that quality back then.

    (looks at the stage)

If we only were patient, who knows what could've happened.

    (snaps back from his deep thoughts and turns to the
    PROPERTY MANAGER)

Yeah I can tell you about Josh and the Phat Kat Lounge. I can tell you all about his tragic love story, and all the wonderful poems that were read here.

THE BLACK WIDOW by Charles Bennett

(the lights lower and the music begins. ZANE and the PROPERTY MANAGER exit the stage and the Phat Kat employees enter, furnishing the bar)

(lights black out)

ACT 1
SCENE 2

(The lights come up on the fully furnished Phat Kat as it was when JOSHUA owned it. ZANE enters the bar; LUCIANO is already there)

ZANE:

What it is Linguini! Where the ladies at dog?

LUCIANO:

It's Luciano, and calm yo'self down, it's still early.

ZANE:

Man what is your real name? I know damn well yo' momma ain't named you some damn Luciano. What's your brother's name, Sergio Valentino?

LUCIANO:

No it's Biff.

ZANE:

What the hell! Man where is Joshua?

LUCIANO:

You know Josh, he is probably tied up with some groupie or writing some new love or sex poem to lure his next victim.

ZANE:

Don't hate the player, hate the game dog. Josh is my man. The
brother ain't balling but he got these women sprung of his poetry. I
wish I had a talent.

LUCIANO:

You do, it's called hustling. What do you got today?

ZANE:

You know me dog. I got it all movies, CDs, video games, whatever. I
even got some porn. Matter fact, I got the classical shit like Scarface,
New Jack City, Friday, and the Passion.

LUCIANO:

You have the nerve to sell bootleg copies of the Passion, Z, you are
going to hell. I bet you got the Passion right next to the porn.

ZANE:

Only Jesus knows my pain and it's called being broke. Mel Gibson
made the Passion and his ass is rich beyond measure. This cat
basically owns Australia. So if Jesus can bless him with a continent,
he could at least bless me with a Benz. (towards the sky) Just a little
Benz Lord! It could be a 2-door or hatchback... (waits) I want the big
body, give me the big body Lord!

LUCIANO:

Z, you are going to hell!

(JOSHUA enters the bar)

JOSHUA:

What ya'll talking about?

ZANE:

My big body Benz that I will one day be blessed with. What's up with you Mr. Love Jones? Why are you so late coming in tonight? You couldn't get your tongue out of the honey jar?

JOSHUA:

Well not really, I had to take Ms. Honey Brown to the airport.

LUCIANO:

Sweet Money Brown. Where is she going?

JOSHUA:

Her group has to perform tomorrow in New York.

LUCIANO:

I didn't know she had a group. What are they called?

JOSHUA:

Shades of Essence.

LUCIANO:

Do you have anybody special coming in tonight to read? Or are you going to steal the show and put some new girl on your roster.

ZANE:

Luciano, don't hate Joshua, he say them words that make them ladies' panties just fall off. Brother you are so smooth with yo' shit. Remember that poem you wrote for me to get my ole lady back. Well it didn't work for her but it worked on Candy, and Candy was so sweet.

(looking at the door)

Man let me get my merchandise so I can make this money in this parking lot. So I can get that big body Benz.

(ZANE walks off to hustle to some customers)

LUCIANO:

Please leave wit yo' lying ass. Joshua, the only reason why I tolerate his crazy ass is because of you. I don't care how cool y'all are but if you don't tell him that my name isn't Linguini I won't let him continue selling that bootleg shit outside in our parking lot. Plus, he never buys anything to drink! We can't make any money if he ain't drinking!

JOSHUA:

Alright man I will talk to him. (sarcastically) So what band you got coming tonight or are you going to be the DJ with the bootleg CDs you bought from ZANE

LUCIANO:

Oh that was cold! You are always taking up for his ass.

(people start coming into the bar)

THE BLACK WIDOW by Charles Bennett

JOSHUA:

Seriously I will talk to him about playing with yo' name, even though you know yo' momma didn't name you Luciano.

LUCIANO:

Whatever hater! Don't get mad at me because my momma gave me a masculine name unlike Joshua or is it Joshie? (laughing). Aye man seriously, I think it's time to get yo' ass on stage and get this party started.

JOSHUA:

(walks onto the stage)

Good evening ladies and gentlemen. My name is Joshua your MC to love, to please, and also to tease on this beautiful night of poetry. If you would like to share some of your poetry please come to the bar and sign your name on the list. Here at the Phat Kat, you can come express yo'self and be accepted. Our groove here is Neo-Soul. A place where you will smell Egyptian musk body oil and sandalwood incense. We don't pressure you to come on stage, because we will always have a couple of poets who are always here and ready to read. The Phat Kat lounge is more than an experience. It's a culture. Until then relax, order some drinks, and please don't forget to tip the barmaids.

(JOSHUA leaves the stage and walks back to the bar. LILY and ROSE enter the bar).

LILY:

Girl this place is laid back and cool as hell. Joshua and Luciano owns the place, and Joshua provides the entertainment. He writes poetry just like you and his poems are so sexy. He's fine too.

ROSE:

Girl, are you his number one fan?

LILY:

Well I admit, I do have somewhat of a crush but I know I am not his type. I wish I was, but just listening to him is just fine for me.

ROSE:

Well, where is this mystery man at? (sarcastically) Your Mr. Love Jones?

JOSHUA:

What's up Lily! you come here so faithfully, are you finally going to get up on the stage and read a poem?

LILY:

Naw, I leave that up to you Mr. Smooth. Joshua, I would like you to meet my cousin Rose. She's from Atlanta and she's a poet, maybe she will read a lil' something tonight.

JOSHUA:

Hello there cutie pie.

ROSE:

Cutie pie is for young girls. I am a grown-ass woman.

JOSHUA:

Well, excuse me Queen!

ROSE:

Well, I would need to be with a King, in order for me to be called a Queen.

JOSHUA:

You just want to be difficult huh!

ROSE:

Isn't that what's life is all about? Being difficult.

JOSHUA:

Yeah, but that's why we learn how to dance during the storms.

ROSE:

Boy bye!

(ROSE and LILY start laughing)

JOSHUA:

OK! I feel you, but if you decide if you want to read just give me a wink. A little something like this:

(JOSHUA gives her a wink)

Let me go up here and bless this mic.

> (walks toward the bar to grab the list and proceeds to the stage).

LILY:

(somewhat angrily) Did he just flirt with you?

ROSE:

Girl he was just running game, but he is cute.

> (looking at JOSHUA)

LILY:

Umm hmm.

> (looking at ROSE with jealousy)

JOSHUA:

Everybody once again welcome to the Phat Kat Lounge and as always ladies we are gonna keep it phat! It's time to bring the first poet up to the stage tonight. Please give it up for my main man Luciano.

> (LUCIANO to the stage)

LUCIANO:

Hello people! First off I just want to say that I am so glad that there is a place like this. A place where you get drunk, hear some artistic shit, and get drunk! (laughing) Seriously, I just want to say thank y'all for

coming tonight, and please bring a friend to poetry night at the Phat
Kat. Now this poem is called "Pen & Paper." Just imagine if the pen
of the poet had feelings. (laughs again) On the real. When a poet
writes some of their saddest poems, or poems dealing with their true
emotions and feelings. That pen becomes very special to them. Ask
any poet if they have a special pen! This poem is about the pen who is
forgotten once the writer falls in love again with the person who
continues to break the writer's heart. The pen who misses their
relationship, only knows it just a matter of time before they will be
reunited. Ladies and gentlemen, "Pen and Paper"!

(JOSHUA, sneaking looks at ROSE, begins writing while
LUCIANO is reading)

You inspire me

You invited me

You reached to me when you were alone

You took me to yo' safest place

Where you do show your face

The darkness corners of yo' home

Now you grabbing me

You exciting me

So girl let's get it on

It's time to confess

So get undress

THE BLACK WIDOW by Charles Bennett

Grab this pen and paper

And do yo' best.

I can hear your anger

I'm no stranger

So please baby baby write on

How could he be creep

Your words are touching me

Every time you change yo' tone

Every time you write

I start to realize

He was the king meant for your throne

But he walked away

That's where I play

So please baby baby write on

You inspire me

You invited me

You reached to me when you were alone

You took me to yo' safest place

Where you do show yo' face

THE BLACK WIDOW by Charles Bennett

The darkness corners of yo' home

Now you grabbing me

You exciting me

So girl let's get it on

It's time to confess

So get undress

Grab this pen and paper

And do yo' best

I know all the things he didn't do

That was special for you

So I can take his place

I hear yo' moans

I know yo' groans

Because you come to me, to release

So keep on writing

Baby keep on fighting

Make this nigga straight R.I.P.

Because when you're done

I'm gonna hear your tongue

THE BLACK WIDOW by Charles Bennett

So please baby speak to me

Why do you cry

Just write goodbye

This man is not what he seems

But he has yo' heart

I just have the dark

Only minutes you spent with me

Now you left me alone

I know it's because of the phone

I bet its him straight begging his plea

Now yo' strokes a lighter

You ain't holding me tighter

So the affair has come to an end

But what he do

When it comes to you

I'll be here until the very end

So when he comes a loss

I'll be the boss

So homeboy piss her off again

THE BLACK WIDOW by Charles Bennett

You inspire me

You invited me

You reach to me when you were alone

You took me to yo' safest place

Where you don't show yo' face

The darkness corners of your home

Now you grabbing me

You exciting me

So girl let's get it on

It's time to confess

So get undress

Grab this pen and paper

And do yo' best.

(JOSHUA walks back to the stage as LUCIANO exits)

JOSHUA:

Luciano that poem was slick. I was feeling that.

(changes to comical style)

Yeah girls, you don't need a man. A man who would desire all that booty, breasts, luscious lips, soft thighs, and give you money. Naw! You don't need that! You got ink! and paper! So you don't need a man, I'm just fine with my pen and pad. So be gone man! I got ink!

THE BLACK WIDOW by Charles Bennett

And paper! (laughing) Luciano you know I'm just playing pimpin'. I really felt that. Poetry was the best therapy for me also during stressed out times and bad relationships. So, I will be reading ya'll a good ass poem later tonight. But the next poet to the mic is Z. Zane is a little rough around the edges, but his poems are stimulating to the mind.

(ZANE shaking his head in approval)

JOSHUA:

So please give it up for Z!

ZANE:

What it do people! What it do! I got a poem for ya'll tonight that is going to have ya'll tripping. I'm not going to tell much about it, I'm just going to jump right in it... ha ha! This poem I got for ya'll is called, "Fuck Me and Just Leave." Also, keep in mind before *y'all* leave, I will be selling bootleg CDs and movies. Now back to my poem, "Fuck Me and Just Leave."

(while ZANE is reading, JOSHUA continues looking at ROSE and writing)

Enter my life and I will show you a world

where a man would cook and bathe his girl.

She advise me to slow down. Long term is

something she said she did not seek,

but her cold-hearted attitude is what attracted me.

THE BLACK WIDOW by Charles Bennett

I figured she was alone.

Just as I.

Beauty that was taken for granted

and no more will she cry.

I asked her could she please save us a dance,

"just one, baby please"

Later that night she came and found me.

I tripped, but I noticed she had interest in me, and

truthfully I've been watching you all night lady.

As the music went from fast to slow.

That's when I got my chance to get in close.

Her hair was black, soft, and smelled so sweet.

Her skin was scented with Victoria Secret.

Love at first sight, bells rang for me.

Then we finally caught eyes, I was trapped, everybody

in the club just disappeared from around me.

I put my hand on her hips,

then I slid them on to her ass.

Took my lips to her ear, flipped it with my

Tongue and she started to laugh.

Then she asked me,

"what's on your mind?"

I whispered in her ear

"Takin' my tongue and licking

you from head to toe.

Licking your thighs, breast, girl

with all this licking, you going to let yourself go.

Shit as a matter of fact. You are going to let it flow

and I hope when I say this you don't think

I am a tootie fruity, but by the end of the night

Girl! I am going to bite you on your booty!"

She said,

"If you really gone do what you say,

come with me back to my house and let me

see what you are really all about."

I gave this girl the best fucking, better than

any woman could receive.

Licking, sucking, different positions, shit I felt

THE BLACK WIDOW by Charles Bennett

like I was the porno king.

As I came for the fourth time, they say

you lose that feeling after you release.

But instead feelings of love was starting

to grow for this lady that was under me.

There is one thing I forgot to mention

because truthfully to repeat it, it always put

a lump in my throat.

After we were finished I decided

I would let her know

that this first night encounter could

grow to be something much mo'!

I leaned over and said,

"Baby you can have all of me,

every night, every day,

just to be in your presence

and you being by my side.

You, being my lady."

She replied and I quote,

"Long term is something I do not seek.

I got my fuck, so now you can leave."

ZANE:

And I'm out y'all. Don't forget I got dat good shit fo' da low low!

(ZANE leaves the stage and JOSHUA grabs the mic.)

JOSHUA:

Please once again give it up to Z. Zane don't take it personal, we all have been victims of lust, but I never had a woman kick me out! Are you sure you wasn't the minute man instead of being the porno king, she did kick you out pimpin'. Let me stop, I got this inspiration to write this poem tonight and I would like to share it with y'all.

(looking directly at ROSE as he reads the title)

It's called… "Loving You From Afar."

I love loving you from afar.

The truth of the matter, I don't even

know who you are?

I like it better this way, once I get to

know you the excitement seems to fade.

I like to hold on to this feeling of curiosity.

It gets me to imagining if you are my destiny.

I love loving you from afar.

THE BLACK WIDOW by Charles Bennett

For me to reach out and touch you,

I would burn because you are a star.

Your whole presence controls my essence, and the

man you are searching for,

I know that I am not even a contestant.

I wonder what comments she would say,

if she knew how she made my heart ache.

I wonder would she cry if I wasn't

sincere and always told her lies?

These are questions that probe my mind,

and thoughts I feel the need to hide.

Fear is what keeps me far,

and a scar that runs so deep in this heart.

I just can't give love another chance,

but my imagination always has you saving me the last dance.

These images I create, baby why disturb this groove.

I know they wouldn't be the same if I got

the chance to know you.

Stand over there... yeah! Real far.

THE BLACK WIDOW by Charles Bennett

Let me admire you and visualize us in the dark.

Two naked bodies searching to reach

the other one's heart,

but I fear if you touched my heart

it would be with a dart.

That's why I love, loving you from afar.

JOSHUA:

Well that's going to wrap it up. Thank you for coming to the Phat Kat tonight. If you are a poet please share your words of rhythmic style with us sometimes here at the Phat Kat. Until then drink, have fun, and don't forget about Z! He got da low low.

(JOSHUA leaves the stage and heads to talk to LUCIANO)

LILY:

I swear girl that poem was for you!

ROSE:

Whatever! Girl it was just a poem, but it was nice and he is sorta smooth with his style. I liked Z's too. I bet they ain't nothing but some hoes.

LILY:

Yeah I know, but Joshua is still humble in his own little way. Why don't you go up there and show him that you are tight with yo' shit.

THE BLACK WIDOW by Charles Bennett

ROSE:

Maybe I will, I will just wait until the next time.

LILY:

You better!

ROSE:

Next time I will read and Joshua will get where I'm coming from. I know he is sexy and cute but I be damn if he thinks a poem will get me to be one of his groupies.

(looking at JOSHUA at the bar)

LILY:

Are you checking him out?

ROSE:

(still looking at JOSHUA)

I mean if he thinks that a poem is going to get me to like him....whatever!

LILY:

Do you like him already?

ROSE:

(looks back at LILY)

Hell no girl, but he has to understand that it takes more than a poem to get my attention.

LILY:

Wait up girl! Joshua is mine. (laughing)

ROSE:

You can have him. (looking back at JOSHUA) Girl let's go, I wonder what grandma has cooked tonight.

(they prepare to leave)

LILY:

Probably gumbo!

(they exit the bar)

LUCIANO:

What's the deal Joshua? That poem was cool, but it was sorta personal. What's the deal?

JOSHUA:

Nothing man. It was just something that move me tonight.

LUCIANO:

What! She had lust in her eyes?

JOSHUA:

Naw! I saw pain but most of all, she seemed lost.

(looking at ROSE as she leaves with LILY)

(lights black out)

THE BLACK WIDOW by Charles Bennett

ACT 2
SCENE 1

(The Phat Kat staff is cleaning the bar as music plays in the
background. The staff talks amongst themselves and start
preparing the bar for the night. LILY and JASMINE enter.)

LILY:

Girl we had ten blunts going around that room.

JASMINE:

What! How many people were over there?

LILY:

About five us, girl I still feel high.

(begins coughing)

JASMINE:

Why are we here so early anyway? I know I haven't been here in
awhile, but damn this is early.

(they sit center stage at a table)

LILY:

I wanted to see if Josh was here yet.

JASMINE:

You still chasing after him? I thought you said he wasn't your type.

LILY:

He ain't, but last night I swear he was checking out my cousin Rose.

JASMINE:

What? Love at first sight, and you have been in his face for years and nothing. I know you are pissed.

LILY:

Well not really. My cousin Rose is weird anyway, she is so damn picky that Josh doesn't stand a chance.

JASMINE:

You hope he doesn't stand a chance.

LILY:

Bitch whatever!

(both start laughing)

JASMINE:

So why do you want to see Joshua?

LILY:

So I can ask him is he digging my cousin before she gets here. She said she was going to read tonight and...

(JASMINE cuts her off)

JASMINE:

And you want to hate on her before she gets here....huh!

LILY:

Yep!

(both start laughing again)

I mean she is just a lame. She hasn't dated since her ex, and she was so damn clingy. That's why he cheated on her bourgeoisie ass.

JASMINE:

But she's your cousin!

LILY:

I wouldn't give a damn if she was my sister, she just can't come up in here and take my man.

JASMINE:

Joshua ain't yours, he never was!

LILY:

He is, he just doesn't know it yet.

JASMINE:

Girl this ain't the Parkers! Just because she gets the professor at the end doesn't mean you have a chance... You crazy bitch.

(both of them laughing)

LILY:

See what I am hoping is that Josh is still messing with that Erykah Badu bitch Honey Brown, if so Rose won't even bother.

THE BLACK WIDOW by Charles Bennett

JASMINE:

But what if he isn't?

LILY:

Well knowing Rose and her hard to get ass, she will give him a hard time and he will just give up.

JASMINE:

But what if Rose starts liking him?

LILY:

Well... I'm gone start hating, but hopefully it won't come to that. Josh will probably come up to me asking about Rose and I will tell him, "yeah, I'll see what's up with that." Then I will tell Rose about Honey Brown and the other women to discourage her from liking him and then..

(JASMINE cuts her off).

JASMINE:

Like I said, bitch you crazy!

LILY:

Shut up hoe!

Fo' real now, Josh will come up to me asking why my cousin is tripping and I will pretend to set up a date and won't tell Rose about it. Josh will think that he got stood up and say forget her and I will be there to comfort him.

JASMINE:

Lily... you smoke too damn much!

LILY:

Yeah I came up with this idea last night.

>(starts laughing and then begins coughing. Her cellphone
>rings)

Hello!... oh what's up boy, I'm at the Phat Kat chillin. Fo'real, oh hell
yeah, I will go to the store now and get the Swisher's. (hangs up) Girl
I'm about to bounce over to Pookie's house, you game?

JASMINE:

I thought you were suppose to wait for Josh so you could start hating
on your cousin?

LILY:

Girl the weed be calling me!

JASMINE:

I can drop you off over at Pookie's, but one of my thugs just got out
and you know what that mean.

LILY:

Yeah five minutes of pleasure. My bad, two minutes, what was I
thinking.

JASMINE:

Whatever hater! Let's go.

(they begin to leave)

LILY:

First let me call my cousin and tell her I can't make it here tonight. I will just tell her that I am starting to feel sick.

JASMINE:

Yeah! Sick in the head.

LILY:

Do you want me to put a voodoo spell on you? My family taught me how to do that shit.

JASMINE:

Don't worry about me, worry about putting one on Joshua.

(LILY stops to find her phone)

Come on cuckoo-bird.

LILY:

Ooh! We got to stop at the corner store first.

(begins coughing and calling ROSE on the phone as they exit the bar)

(lights black out)

ACT 2
SCENE 2

(The stage is lit. LUCIANO is talking to a deliveryman)

LUCIANO:

Just put the shipment in the back. Thanks Ron.

(JOSHUA enters)

Well Joshua, is that you, I see from afar?

JOSHUA:

Ha, ha, funny. What's up?

LUCIANO:

Nothing much, just got these shipment orders to take care of. What's up with you? You never here this early.

JOSHUA:

My next door neighbor was blasting his music and I thought I would come here and do some writing.

LUCIANO:

Trying to impress Lily's cousin? What is her name?

JOSHUA:

Rose, was I that obvious?

LUCIANO:

Yeah! Lily looked sort of pissed that you were digging her.

JOSHUA:

I don't know why? Lily smokes too much weed for me, I hope her cousin isn't a pothead.

LUCIANO:

Naw! Her lips wasn't black enough. So what are you working on?

JOSHUA:

Just a little something for my new eye candy, but I don't know what to write because I haven't heard her read yet. I want to feel her vibe before I start writing.

LUCIANO:

(sarcastically) Hopefully she will read something so you can get your inspiration.

JOSHUA:

Ha ha you are just full of jokes tonight.

LUCIANO:

Well I'm just getting ready for Z's ass.

(ZANE enters)

And speaking of the devil himself!

ZANE:

Linguini you were thinking of me?

LUCIANO:

Joshua!

ZANE:

Man I'm just playing. Joshua, word on the street is that you are sprung on Lily's cousin off first sight. What's the deal pimpin'?

JOSHUA:

What!

ZANE:

Yeah Lily and I was just smoking. I was over Pookie's selling some movies and she was saying, I hope Josh isn't feeling my cousin like that because she hasn't gotten over her ex. She said she had to get away from her tonight because she was getting on her nerves going on about some old dude. What's the deal, playboy?

JOSHUA:

Man I'm just playing it cool like always. Playing it cool, I like how that sounds.

LUCIANO:

There you go playboy.

JOSHUA:

Ya'll gonna have to excuse me. I feel a poem coming over me.

(JOSHUA takes a seat and starts writing)

ZANE:

Man what the hell happen last night?

LUCIANO:

Man yo' boy saw Lily's cousin and he's been tripping ever since.

ZANE:

What's up with Ms. Honey Brown?

LUCIANO:

Your guess is good as mine.

ZANE:

I mean, I don't see nothing wrong with getting yo'self a lil side piece, but by him hosting a poetry night where these two ladies could meet face to face, it's going to be some drama. I just hope he knows what he is doing. He better be careful messing around with them Louisiana women.

(JOSHUA walks by and hears ZANE's last comment about ROSE)

JOSHUA:

Rose isn't from Louisiana, she's from Atlanta. The South, I can use that in my poem.

THE BLACK WIDOW by Charles Bennett

(JOSHUA walks to this office to write and Rose enters the bar)

ROSE:

Am I too early?

LUCIANO:

Somewhat, but you can hang out for awhile. Where is Lily?

ROSE:

She wasn't feeling good, so I decided to come by myself.

LUCIANO:

(under his breath) Probably from smoking all that damn weed.

ROSE:

Can I sign the list now?

(JOSHUA comes out of his office and seems amazed to see ROSE)

Yeah, sure let me find the clipboard.

JOSHUA:

Well hello there! Are going to bless us with your lovely voice tonight?

ZANE:

Oh boy.

(Sits at the bar with his back turned as if he is not listening)

ROSE:

Yeah, I got a little something.

JOSHUA:

Well Rose, I can't wait to hear your poem. I know it will be a masterpiece such as yourself.

(they stare at each other smiling. People start coming into the bar)

LUCIANO:

OK! Let's get the club ready for tonight.

(JOSHUA makes ROSE a drink brings it to her)

JOSHUA:

The first drink is on me.

ROSE:

Thank you Joshua.

(they stare at each other smiling)

ZANE:

Well I see it's about time for me to work on that Benz, I will check y'all two cats out later.

(ZANE exits)

LUCIANO:

Joshua, I think it's about time for you to get on the mic.

JOSHUA:

(breaks off drinking with ROSE, caught off base)

Yeah... OK! Let me get ready.

(JOSHUA walks onto the stage)

Ladies and gentlemen how is everyone feeling tonight at the Phat Kat? It's about that time to get this night started so if you want to share your words please sign the list.

(JOSHUA leaves the stage and goes to the bar while checking out ROSE. JOSHUA grabs the list and heads back to the stage.)

OK! I see on the list that we have some new-comers tonight. Our regulars are missing in action and that's cool. I will start tonight's poetry reading with my new piece, "I'm Going To Play It Cool." I hope ya'll enjoy this one.

I'm going to play it cool.

I'm not going to cut up or get rude.

I'm just going to play the background until

everything is smooth.

I want you and this is no lie.

I fiend for you, but you will never see

that in my eyes.

I only known you for a few days,

but already I feel

I known you all my life.

I am going to watch the days go by

which end up in weeks.

Every hour I desire you more, but

I will figure out when it's the

right time for me to speak.

So I'm going to play it cool,

but damn girl I do want you.

But if I act on my feelings I might

look like a fool.

So I'm going to sit back and just

watch you, study how you walk.

The way you slide your fingers through your hair,

and I imagine my fingers being there.

I imagine you as a fragrance, naw fuck that, a fruit!

As I caress you in my hands, I'm gentle for I

do not want you to bruise.

My eyes open wide as I pull you

THE BLACK WIDOW by Charles Bennett

closer to my mouth.

I bet you are as sweet as a Georgia peach!

Since you are from the South.

As my lips touch your outer skin they get moist.

Anticipating the freaky things that I want to do.

As my lips crack you open your juices begin to flow.

As I bite, nibble, you yearn for me to

devour you even more.

As I lick my lips for the last time,

and open my eyes to come

down from this high.

I realize for now all I can do is wait.

I don't know what to say?

I even don't know what to do?

So in meanwhile, I'm just going to play it cool.

(JOSHUA pauses for applause)

JOSHUA:

Thank you. OK next we have one of our newcomers, and ya'll better treat her right and show her some love. I bring ya'll the most beautiful flower of them all... Rose!

(ROSE comes to the stage not looking at JOSHUA)

ROSE:

Hello people, I'm kinda shy but I'm not scared to share this poem with ya'll.

(she clears her throat and gets ready)

This poem is called, "Until That Day."

They say when you reach a certain age

it's time to stop the play,

the game,

the chase.

To just give in and just have faith.

I've yet to meet that face.

So, until that day.

They say your whole purpose of life is to create.

Give birth, not just once but twice.

To raise a family,

to care and provide

and be a loving and caring wife.

Then why is that starting to seem like a myth,

some type of bold face lie.

THE BLACK WIDOW by Charles Bennett

Why does it have to be this way.

So, until that day.

I'm going to hold back.

They say that true love is only a myth,

but true love is the only kiss.

True love is my only bliss.

True love is what I really miss.

They say settle down and do what's right.

Meet a man with financial stability,

marry him and become his wife

Not I.

If I have to live alone,

then shit is on!

I will know when the moment is right.

I will know it when I finally see those eyes.

I will know when I will meet that one

who I will cherish for life.

So until then. Let me wait. Let me pray.

THE BLACK WIDOW by Charles Bennett

Let me stay true.

Until that day.

(Applause. ROSE leaves the stage and JOSHUA returns to the mic)

JOSHUA:

Ohh! I mean next we have another new newcomer to the mic. Terrance, step to the mic and share your words!

(TERRANCE comes on stage)

TERRANCE:

Hello everybody, I wrote this poem when I was in college. You hear so many couples complain about their lovers back home. Missing them. Wanting them. Especially my old roommate. He was always talking about his girl back home. So I would like to share this poem that I wrote in secret about him. It's called, "A Trick 4 Tonight."

(while TERRANCE reads, JOSHUA is at the bar writing frantically)

You deserve to be treated right,

a woman needs to respect you, hold you

and constantly remind you how she is

happy to have you in her life.

But there is one thing, I want you, but

I don't want you to be mine.

THE BLACK WIDOW by Charles Bennett

I've been wondering since you say you are

lonely, could I be your trick for tonight?

I don't want a relationship, my heart has

had enough of that emotional ride.

I just want to hold you, caress you, and fantasize

for one night that you are forever mine.

You say that your woman is back home.

That's so far away.

So tonight only tonight can I please take her place?

Can I do to you those tricks that you love?

Can I do some new tricks that your woman has not even thought of?

Does she ever take the time to use her creativity

before ya'll get into the act of making love.

Does she use whip cream, fruit, and ice, to assist her

when she is using her tongue?

Does your woman satisfy your every need?

Is she so freaky that she would take off your

draws with her teeth?

Does she massage your body with her

THE BLACK WIDOW by Charles Bennett

hands and oils?

When her tongue is gliding up your

thigh, does yo' blood boil?

She gives you none of these privileges,

these pleasures she denies.

So I'm asking you boy to think.

Just to be with her you had to make a sacrifice.

So come home with me,

be with a trick for one night.

I would understand if you hesitate.

An act like this a man must take time

to probe his mind.

So before I leave, and I finally say goodbye.

I was wondering since you say you are

Lonely,

could I be your trick for tonight?

TERRANCE:

I hope ya'll enjoyed that.

THE BLACK WIDOW by Charles Bennett

(the crowd is dead silent until one of TERRANCE's friends stands up and starts clapping. TERRANCE rejoins his friends at their table.)

LUCIANO:

(taps JOSHUA who looks up, startled)

Did you just hear that shit?

JOSHUA:

What! He's just in love with men.

LUCIANO:

That dude just read some gay shit and you like whatever?

JOSHUA:

So! A man gots to do what a man gots to do.

(walks back to the stage)

I must share this poem with ya'll. It's called, "Have You Ever."

Have you ever loved a woman at first sight?

She was so tight, yo' dream,

Your vision finally come to life.

You see this fantasy has now become reality,

and so she speaks

and it's so sweet.

Have you ever loved a woman,

THE BLACK WIDOW by Charles Bennett

in just one day, and night you prayed

Lord make her stay.

You say I finally found her,

my life has begun today.

Have you ever met the most beautifulness

thing on earth, kissed her and

all you could think,

I want this woman to be the mother of my child.

I want her to be the first.

To give birth.

Have you?

Well I met the woman who could make my soul cry.

Who made me feel like I wanted to die.

Who made me want to give up on life.

Shit I met her twice.

To meet her again,

I would do it all over my friend.

Because that's love.

It sweeps you off your feet.

THE BLACK WIDOW by Charles Bennett

It makes you meek.

It makes you sweet.

The truth,

sometimes it only lasts about a week.

Ya'll know what I mean.

But have you ever thought

you met the lady of

your dreams.

JOSHUA:

Well people, that's going to do it for tonight. Please drive home safely and please come back to the Phat Kat where we always keep it nice and phat for y'all.

(JOSHUA walks back to the bar)

LUCIANO:

Man this spot ain't for no freaking homos to come in and make a whorehouse out of. Soon this spot will be full of fudge-packers.

(starts humping the air)

This spot is called the Phat Kat! Get it Phat Kat!

(ZANE enters the bar)

JOSHUA:

That is true, but remember it's a place where people come to express their true feelings in an artistic form. That's all, Luciano... that's all.

(JOSHUA walks to ROSE, center-stage on a couch, and sits across from her on the other couch.)

ROSE:

So Joshua, have you met her lately?

JOSHUA:

Yes! I believe I have!

ROSE:

Oh really!

JOSHUA:

Would you like to go down the street and get a flan?

ROSE:

What's that?

JOSHUA:

It's custard, a sweet dessert . This Puerto Rican restaurant makes the best flans I ever had. It's just down the street.

ROSE:

They got food there? Because I usually eat dessert after dinner. I'm not going to front! A sister is hungry!

THE BLACK WIDOW by Charles Bennett

JOSHUA:

Yeah! They got food there. So what's up? Would you like to go, so I can feed you girl!

ROSE:

Yeah that would be nice.

(they exit together)

(lights black out)

ACT 2
SCENE 3

(Lights come up. ZANE and LUCIANO are sitting at the
bar. REGGIE enters.)

REGGIE:

So did y'all miss me? Chocolate thunder is back!

LUCIANO:

Reggie, what's up man! Yo' ass miss poetry night last night, and man
was it crazy!

REGGIE:

What! Did Honey Brown perform last night?

ZANE:

Naw, but *he* was sweet like honey.

REGGIE:

What the hell are y'all talking about?

LUCIANO:

Remember back in high school. When we were at the Cleveland
School of the Arts. We had a lot of homosexuals. Well, this guy
named Terrance read last night, and represented for the LGBTQ
community.

ZANE:

Man, why in the hell does their organization has that long ass title of letters. If you were trying to cuss one of them out! By the time you finished saying all them damn letters, you've forgotten what the hell you was going to say.

REGGIE:

Wow! So the Phat Kat is a LGBTQ spot now?

LUCIANO:

Naw, but if it brings money! I'll think about it. I'm checking Facebook and Instagram to read people comments to see if this helped or damaged the Phat Kat. Can't be fucking wit my money.

REGGIE:

As long as Honey Brown can still come. I don't really give a shit!

ZANE:

Luciano, you and money! Is that all you think about?

LUCIANO:

Hell yes! If you had an ex-wife killing yo' ass with alimony and child support, you would be too! After we divorce, I swear it felt like I married a gold digger. It was all about the checks and child support. My ex-wife became my baby mama baby drama.

REGGIE:

Oh, that's why you wrote that poem back in the day?

ZANE:

What poem? Let me hear this shit.

LUCIANO:

I know that damn poem by heart. Fuck it, what the hell.

(takes the stage)

I got this baby momma

I got this baby drama

I got this woman who would

Do nothing but cold stop me

For having fun

For getting some

She always think that I

Got some pussy on my tongue

I just got to let you know

Homie I'm pro

And I ain't going to let this woman

Just stop my flow

I love that heavy metal

I love that rock n roll

I love anything that gets my ass

THE BLACK WIDOW by Charles Bennett

Out of control

But then she rings my cell

And I'm like what the hell

What drama she got to fucking tell

Sometimes she makes me pissed

But I think about my child

And that's the only person that I want to kiss

So I take her shit

But deep in my mind yo I'm tired of this

I got that baby momma

I got that baby drama

I got this shit that will cold haunt you

And ever since I took my leave

She has been threatening me

With all that bullshit that use to scare me

Like child support

Like going to court

But I give her money for my child's support

But it ain't enough

THE BLACK WIDOW by Charles Bennett

I just wanna get rough

Man I'm sick and tired of her fucking bluffs

I got this baby momma

I got that baby drama

I got this chick

Who will do nothing but cold rob me

Of my life

Of my seed

If we had love

Shit, I just can't believe

Because all I see

That was in her tummy

Was her way of getting some fucking money

I don't mean no disrespect

But when we named our child

We should've just named him Check!

I got this baby momma

I got this baby drama

THE BLACK WIDOW by Charles Bennett

Homie I, I, I,

I got fucking drama.

ZANE:

Damn, so that's why you are always pressed about money.

LUCIANO:

By the time her lawyers got done with me, I was flat broke. If it wasn't for Josh, I don't know how I would've made it.

REGGIE:

I always wondered how you and Josh became business partners. Did he go to school with us too?

LUCIANO:

Naw. He went to Cleveland Heights, I met Josh at Alabama State University. I was a junior and Josh was a freshman. We were both business and marketing majors. Cynthia and I had just started dating, and she wanted to go to this poetry reading on campus. Josh got on the mic and said he was from Cleveland before he read his poem. When you are in school out of state, you get pumped to meet somebody who's from your hometown. Josh and I got cool, and he told me all about his life. Both of his parents died in a car accident when he was thirteen. His grandmother raised him after they passed, and she died his senior year in high school.

ZANE:

Damn, I didn't know all that.

LUCIANO:

After college, Cynthia and I got married. Moved to her hometown in Berkeley, California. We had two kids and I got caught cheating. I moved back to Cleveland, and was at a poetry spot and there was Josh. I told him what happened and all he said was, "Are you still alive? Then let's get that money for your family."

ZANE:

He said the same shit to me. You must be talking about that poetry spot in Cleveland Heights called the B-Side. My daughter's mother and I had just broke up. Man I couldn't keep a job for nothing due to my drinking. Once she left me, the pain of not seeing my daughter every morning turned me into a bona fide acholic. Man, I was in so much pain. Trying to live that single life hitting club after club. Searching for a woman to replace my girl, but I knew no woman could replace her. So I was on that bottle.

(goes on stage)

Since we are reading poems. I will read the poem I read that night. It's called, "I'm in a Club, But I'm Chilling at the Bar."

50 dollars!

That's all that I have,

So mix me up something real tasty

Something real bad.

She said mister. Mister please,

I got something that will drop you down to your knees.

THE BLACK WIDOW by Charles Bennett

Creamy on top, and deep down inside

Boy let me stop!

I said Miss!

I was being polite at this time

So I said this with a kiss,

Give it to me

I'm in need for a fix.

She said something strong?

I said all night long.

She said don't worry boo,

I see you are hurting, so I'm gone take care of you.

This bartender,

Cocoa was her name

Made me decide to chill

And ride out my stay.

Soon, it will be the last call for alcohol

And I need something to drink

So I won't think at all.

I'm in a club

THE BLACK WIDOW by Charles Bennett

But I'm chilling at the bar.

Now every club has a Cocoa

Wise, intriguing, divine

A star!

Every club has a Cocoa bartending at the bar

She gives you bits and pieces of her life.

Her glory, misfortunes, desires, and pain.

She becomes more than just a cute face

She becomes a woman with a name

You find yourself smiling

When she comes around.

You find yourself laughing a little louder

(Girl I don't need no coffee)

When she comes around

Makes you think

If I listen to my girl a lot closer

Maybe she would come around.

To all the Cocoa's

Non-licensed psychiatrist giving free advice

THE BLACK WIDOW by Charles Bennett

At your local neighborhood bar.

Can spot a man who's having troubles at home

And matters concerning the heart.

When a man is down and reached his final low.

The club is where he will go,

And that's where he will find someone like Cocoa

And like his woman

She will tell him when his drinking

Has gone to damn far!

Like I said,

I'm in a club, but I'm chilling at the bar!

REGGIE:

So that's how you met Joshua. I live in Cleveland Heights now, and I have been to that spot a few times to read. Over there off of Coventry.

LUCIANO:

So that's why you never drink? I always thought you were just broke!

(all laughing)

ZANE:

Yeah! Once I got finished with my poem, I went outside to get ready to sell my CDs and movies. I must've had too much to drink that night because I started throwing up. After I cleant myself up, I saw

Josh standing right next to me. He said, "Are you still alive? Well, let's get you off that bottle for your family." I didn't know what to say. I was like who the hell is this guy. Next thing I know, I'm telling this dude all my problems. That liquor had me running my damn mouth until I was about to start crying. Then Josh punk ass broke the tension by giving me a nickname.

REGGIE:

Well! What's the damn nickname?

ZANE:

I will never tell that damn nickname! I'm taking that shit to my grave. All I can tell you is, my daughter's mother is a Puerto Rican.

(REGGIE and LUCIANO at the same time:)
Ahhshit!

ZANE:

Yeah! One time, we were arguing and she grab a knife. So I grabbed a bigger knife. Man, her eyes lit up with excitement, and she came charging at me.

REGGIE:

What the hell did you do?

ZANE:

Screamed and ran like a bitch!

(all laughing)

THE BLACK WIDOW by Charles Bennett

Man, I miss her crazy ass. Anyways, Josh told me that he was going into business with his old friend and opening up a bar. He said I could come there and sell my shit, but come sober. So I came clean and sober. Josh gave me three hundred dollars and told me to go check on my daughter and her mother. He said he would continue to help me out as long as I stayed sober. I been here ever since.

REGGIE:

Man! All I came here for was to ask when was the next time Honey Brown is coming back. Y'all two, and these damn reminiscing stories. Z! First off, you need to let the bootleg CDs and movies go. You ain't heard of the internet? It shut the game down bruh. I'm a substitute teacher for Cleveland public schools, and them iPhones and Galaxies sell like crack! Well, when crack was the shit. Anyways, invest in some iPhones and Galaxies. You and yo' baby momma will thank me. Now! Is Honey Brown coming back anytime soon?

LUCIANO:

(shaking his head)

Yeah man. She'll be back.

REGGIE:

That's all a brother wanted to know.....damn!

(Lights black out.)

THE BLACK WIDOW by Charles Bennett

ACT 3
SCENE 1

(JOSHUA at the bar talking to barmaid TIFFANY)

JOSHUA:

I really am starting to like this girl. She's different, and I do believe I'm starting to fall for her.

TIFFANY:

I see, but Josh don't rush it.

JOSHUA:

Yeah, I really don't have that much luck when it comes to love. That game I always lose. So maybe I need to relax huh?

TIFFANY:

Joshua, all I know is that you have a lot of girls that you go through. I knew sooner or later that somebody would get your attention to slow you down. I thought Honey Brown was the one, but I guess I was wrong.

JOSHUA:

She's cool, but she's not looking for love. She is what you call a free spirit. She just goes with the flow, and that's what I like about her.

TIFFANY:

Oh! Somebody who you can fuck without any strings attached?

JOSHUA:

Yeah I guess, but it's not like that. She's very much into the arts, and poetry is her first love. She wants to make it a career and take her group Shades of Essence to the mainstream of entertainment. She's not looking for a relationship and I understand that. She comes here for exposure and to practice out some new material before she takes her group to the big cities. We just meet and hit it off.

TIFFANY:

Oh, you just got it like that huh!

JOSHUA:

Not really. Well maybe just a little.

(laughing as ROSE enters)

ROSE:

Hello Joshua.

JOSHUA:

What's up Rose, I was just thinking about you.

(TIFFANY pardons herself and continues cleaning)

ROSE:

Oh really, I just wanted to thank you for a nice evening last night.

JOSHUA:

Anytime Rose, I would love to cook you dinner sometime. Maybe some steak, lobster, shrimp. Whatever you like.

THE BLACK WIDOW by Charles Bennett

ROSE:

(Pauses)... How about we go to a restaurant instead?

JOSHUA:

(Pauses).....OK. That I can do.

ROSE:

I guess you are wondering why I stop by.

JOSHUA:

Well yeah, but I'm just happy I got the chance to see you again.

ROSE:

Josh can you make me a drink?

JOSHUA:

You had a hard day today?

ROSE:

I want to ask you something.

JOSHUA:

What's up?

ROSE:

I've heard this and that about you, and I just want to hear what you have to say about yourself.

JOSHUA:

What do you want to know?

(hands her a drink and makes one for himself)

ROSE:

Are you a player? Do you think I am some girl that you are going to put on your hit list. Tell all your boys, "yeah I hit that pimpin'." Huh! Is that your game Joshua?

JOSHUA:

Rose you got me pegged all wrong. That's not my style!

ROSE:

What is your style then?

JOSHUA:

You!

ROSE:

That was lame!

(ROSE looks JOSHUA straight in the eyes)

Really the truth.

JOSHUA:

When I was in college, I had this image of what my perfect girl should be. I dated athletes, cheerleaders, sorority girls and so on. No matter what they did they were all the same. They wanted the

THE BLACK WIDOW by Charles Bennett

basketball player, football player, or the guy who came from money. I was always told you will meet your wife in college. Well most girls in college aren't looking for husbands. What they are looking for is a good time.

ROSE:

That's true because if you and the guy aren't from the same city, it's hard to make a relationship work after graduation. Was that the case for you?

JOSHUA:

Not really! I was crazy for this girl who was a cheerleader. She was majoring in education. I was with her for 3 years and right around my last year she decided to call it off.

ROSE:

What, the relationship?

JOSHUA:

No! Marriage! We were suppose to get married once I graduated. I finished school, but she married the quarterback of our college football team.

ROSE:

That had to be painful.

JOSHUA:

Our last year together she got pregnant with my baby. She wanted to get an abortion because she wasn't ready and plus she would lose her scholarship because she was a cheerleader. I wanted her to keep our baby, but what could I do. Her mind was made up and she aborted the baby. From then on she made me wear protection so that wouldn't happen again. After we broke up, I found out the reason why she aborted the baby. While we were together, she was fucking the quarterback on road-trips. Once she found out she was pregnant she didn't know for sure who's baby it was, and she wanted to make sure it was his. Right before my graduation, I found out that she was pregnant again. This time she was sure it was his.

ROSE:

Well maybe since she was done with school it was OK for her to be pregnant. Being pregnant in school was probably too much for her to handle.

JOSHUA:

No! She had one more year of school left. He graduated with me, but he got drafted to the Houston Texans. So I guess that made it OK. Love had nothing to do about it when it came to destroying my baby. Money did. I wasn't guaranteed. I thought we had love, I thought I was special. She dropped out of school and moved to Houston Texas with him.

ROSE:

You mean to tell me she got pregnant twice in one year?

JOSHUA:

Yeah! I felt so stupid at graduation. Everybody knew that we had just broke up and now she was pregnant. I never told anyone that she was pregnant with my child just months earlier. I didn't even bother going to any graduation parties. I had my bags packed in my car, and right after graduation I left.

ROSE:

So how long has it been since you got into another relationship?

JOSHUA:

About three years now. I thought she really loved me, I thought she was the one. After that I just became a hoe! Fuck-em and leave-em was my motto. But eventually that gets old because everybody needs someone to love. I miss it! I miss being in love and loving someone back. Even if it isn't real. That feeling has you waking every morning like hell yeah! I am somebody! (chuckles)

ROSE:

Yeah! I miss being in love too.

(they look at each other)

JOSHUA:

It's nothing like love. Sex is one thing, but love...

(staring into ROSE's eyes)

ROSE:

It's special.

(ROSE gets closer to JOSHUA)

JOSHUA:

Yeah.

(they stop and look at each other)

ROSE:

So you said you were going to cook me steak, lobster, shrimp and whatever else? (starts to giggle)

JOSHUA:

(talking sexy) Whatever you like Rose.

ROSE:

You got any wine?

JOSHUA:

I'm part owner of a bar, what do you think.

(they both start to laugh as LILY enters the bar)

ROSE:

Maybe I might take you up on that offer? I am sort of hungry!

JOSHUA:

Rose if you want to talk, eat, and all, just call me.

(JOSHUA goes into his office; employees continue cleaning the bar)

LILY:

Oh so you have a date for tonight?

THE BLACK WIDOW by Charles Bennett

ROSE:

He wants me to come over for dinner but I don't know.

LILY:

Girl if you think I am tripping over Josh liking you, you're wrong.

ROSE:

I thought you might be jealous, but I wanted to ask him up front what were his intentions.

LILY:

Girl whatever. Joshua ain't nothing but a hoe, so you better be careful if you decide to go over there.

ROSE:

I will keep that in mind, but are you sure you're not mad because...

(LILY cuts her off)

LILY:

Girl do whatever you want. Like I said, I knew I wasn't his type, so I never thought that he would ask me out. So give him a shot, but just be careful because he's a dog. Anyways how could I compare to you, I'm just a lily and you are a rose. The only thing I attract are frogs. Get it, lily pads and frogs. Go over there! Shit it's a free meal.

ROSE:

Maybe I will, I don't know.

LILY:

Girl go, just remember he's a hoe so keep those legs crossed.

ROSE:

You bet I will.

LILY:

Let's go find you something to wear for your hot date.

ROSE:

Oh girl stop it!

(ROSE goes to the door ready to leave but LILY hangs back looking at JOSHUA, who doesn't notice. All lights out except a spot on LILY)

LILY:

I hate you Joshua!

(back to usual lighting)

ROSE:

Lily! You coming?

LILY:

Yeah girl!

(lights black out)

ACT 4
SCENE 1

(LUCIANO is sweeping the floor as JOSHUA enters the bars)

JOSHUA:

I thought we had employees for that?

LUCIANO:

Oh what's up man, I was bored and decided to do it myself. Have you checked the figures for this month? Man we are doing good!

(JOSHUA yells over his shoulder as he gets to his office)

JOSHUA:

Naw, I've been busy.

LUCIANO:

Yeah busy with Rose. You have been with her every day this week.

JOSHUA:

Yeah!

(smiling, facing LUCIANO again)

I have gotten attached to her, she's different. She has a sense of humor, she's sexy as hell, and we have the most deepest stimulating conversations I ever had with a woman.

LUCIANO:

Oh ya'll haven't done the nasty yet I take it?

JOSHUA:

Nope!

(both laughing)

LUCIANO:

Stimulating conversations. Negro please!

JOSHUA:

Man that's what I like about her. I don't want to rush this right now. I'm just enjoying the moment, but I wouldn't mind tapping that ass!

(ZANE enters)

ZANE:

Hee hee.....What ya'll girls laughing about?

LUCIANO:

Joshua's horny ass.

ZANE:

Oh so you haven't slept with Lily's cousin yet. Poor thing!

JOSHUA:

Man ya'll a trip! I came here to get my cell phone charger out of the office, and all ya'll heathens can do is talk about sex. Both of ya'll are going to hell.

THE BLACK WIDOW by Charles Bennett

(JOSHUA goes into his office)

ZANE:

You know you want them draws, so nigga stop acting. What's up with you, Linguini, I got them movies and CDs you wanted. Do you want to see my adult collection? Huh... huh.

LUCIANO:

I swear if you wasn't JOSHUA's boy and didn't have shit I need --

(pauses to think about Z's last comment)

Let me see what you got.

JOSHUA:

(comes out of his office)

Well I see ya'll later.

ZANE:

Going to hook up with Rose?

JOSHUA:

Yeah, we are supposed to go to a comedy show and then back to my place.

LUCIANO:

Do your thing pimpin'.

(JOSHUA exits)

ZANE:

Check this out dog.

(open his bag of porno movies)

LUCIANO:

(looking inside the bag) Oh man, you got Asian chicks, Latin chicks, and black chicks!

ZANE:

Pimpin', I got big booty white girls too!

LUCIANO:

(Looking at the box) Dammmmmmnnn!

(lights black out)

ACT 5
SCENE 1

(Lights come up and ROSE is sitting on JOSHUA's lap on the couch. The club isn't open yet and there's no staff or customers)

JOSHUA:

Come on! Stop acting so shy. With all that mouth you got! Yo' ass is far from shy.

ROSE:

Shut up boy. I'm just nervous that you might not respond like I want you to.

JOSHUA:

What! Girl just read the poem.

ROSE:

OK, but I want you to be honest when I ask you how you feel after I'm finished.

(she grabs a sheet of paper out of her pocket)

It's called, "It Grows."

Eternal bliss.

A sweet kiss.

Days I dreamt, but never

did I think it would

be like this.

Let me start by saying I admit

I didn't know.

But when you find the right person

they just glow.

The feeling you feel it takes control.

When it comes to love it just

doesn't happen,

it grows.

It started with a simple attraction.

As we started to talk,

I saw a spark.

That didn't trigger my lust, but my heart.

Love is romance.

Love is taking a chance.

Love is knowing he will always save you the last dance.

Love happens after the first glance.

So now I wait.

Love is a gamble,

THE BLACK WIDOW by Charles Bennett

who gives a damn about mistakes.

Like I said,

I didn't know.

But when it comes to love,

it just doesn't happen.

It continues to grow.

(ROSE looks at JOSHUA wanting to hear what he has to say)

JOSHUA:

Man that was deep.

ROSE:

Oh hell naw, you gonna tell me more than just deep!

JOSHUA:

Rose, I'm tired of being hurt. Yes, these past few weeks has been magical. We click so good, but most girls play with me and then put me down. Then I'm the one who is brokenhearted. Yeah girls love to hear cute poems, but poems doesn't pay the bills. Poems don't buy cars and jewelry. Poetry is my therapy and right now therapy ain't paying.

ROSE:

I'm not like that.

(ROSE gets off JOSHUA's lap)

THE BLACK WIDOW by Charles Bennett

JOSHUA:

I've heard that line plenty of times. Rose, please let's just take this slow. Not because I don't care about you in that way but...

(ROSE cuts him off)

ROSE:

Naw, because yo' ass want to fuck as many women as you can because you've been hurt. Stop making excuses and be a man and take this as a challenge. So what, you meet some gold-digging hood rats that broke your heart. Yes, you have a good heart and a kind spirit and certain women took advantage of that. But I'm real and my feelings don't change like the seasons. I just opened my heart to you. I care for you and I would love to see this grow, but I see it's hard to make a boy who wants to play grow into a man.

(heading to the door)

JOSHUA:

Rose... Rose please!

ROSE:

Oh Joshua save it! Why don't you go write a poem about it. Honestly Josh! What is it that you see in me? What made me get your attention? Why do you even like me Joshua?

JOSHUA:

OK Rose, you want the truth! Yes, I am sitting on a shit load of
money. Being my parents' only child, and my grandmother's only
grandson. Losing my parents was the hardest and saddest event of my
life. Coming back from a vacation, my parents stopped at a rest area
off the freeway. A truck driver who fell asleep behind the wheel
pulling into the rest area slammed into their car. My wealth has been
gained on losing my family. That money will only be spent on my
future family. Susan only got pregnant to spend my money. When the
offer came to get with a future NFL player, she aborted my baby.
Truthfully I wasn't surprised, I saw greed and deception in her eyes,
but I overlooked it. She was beautiful, and I wanted to be wrong just
to start a family. So when you ask me, what was it about you that got
my attention? What is it about you that made me like you? The pain I
saw in your eyes. I saw it with Zane, and I saw it with Luciano. Most
importantly, I saw it in myself. I believe we have something in
common. I believe we both are searching for love to replace that
sadness. I could be wrong, but I swear I see that in your eyes. I
thought maybe this time I could help you and you could help me. We
could work together to rid ourselves from our sadness. Maybe I'm
just getting caught up again, and that's why I don't want to rush
anything.

ROSE:

No... Joshua, you are right. There is sadness in these eyes. I lost my
parents too Joshua. Unlike your parents, it wasn't a vacation. My
father was very abusive to my mother. Finally after one severe
beating that left her with a cracked skull, she decided enough was

THE BLACK WIDOW by Charles Bennett

enough. I was a freshmen in high school and they had an audition for the play, "The Wiz" after school. I remember as a child, I would always pick the "The Wiz" to watch for popcorn Friday night's. My father would always try to sing the Lion's part. He was so horrible, but we were happy. I wanted to surprise my mother if I got a part in the play. I didn't tell her and I would be late coming home from school. When I got home the police were at my house. They told me that my father had killed my mother and himself. All I could think was, what if I was home too. I moved in with my mother's older sister Ann and was haunted with the fact that I could've been dead too. I vowed to never get into an abusive relationship, but I did. My ex-boyfriend use words and mind games to abuse me. He kept me away from my aunt, claiming she never liked him. After she passed away from breast cancer, all I had was him in Atlanta. That's when the head games began. I was plainand unattractive to him. My cooking and house cleaning was never to his standards. I was at Clark Atlanta studying to be a teacher and by the grace of God I made it through. My love for children and student teaching was an escape from my depression. After graduation, I noticed my period was late. I went home and cooked a big dinner for Lucas. I had the dining room table all set with candles and my mother's fine china. Lucas came home late smelling like booze and perfume. He took his plate and threw it in the garbage. I sat at that table praying to God please don't let me be pregnant by this man. The next day my period came and I decided enough was enough. I called my grandmother who was now living here in Cleveland because her and my mother's youngest sister Gladys lost their homes during Katrina. So I left Atlanta and all the bad memories behind. So yes Joshua, I do have pain in my eyes. We do have something in common.

THE BLACK WIDOW by Charles Bennett

JOSHUA:

I'm glad you came to Cleveland. They always say the grass is greener on the other side.

ROSE:

That might be true, but here in Cleveland!

(they both laugh, breaking the tension between them)

JOSHUA:

Why you gotta be talking shit about my city. Maybe we could plant a field together. We could nurture and love it all your round. We could grow some little roses and some marijuana. Whatever you want baby.

ROSE:

Why you gotta be stupid.

JOSHUA:

(Walking up to ROSE)

Seriously, let's grow together. You and I, let's plant a garden.

(LUCIANO enters)

LUCIANO:

Oh, did I come in at a bad time.

ROSE:

No, I was just leaving. Joshua I will talk to you later. I hope you have a green thumb.

THE BLACK WIDOW by Charles Bennett

(They kiss goodbye and ROSE exits.)

LUCIANO:

Joshua! You are playing a dangerous game. Do you really want Rose? Do you really want a girlfriend? Do you honestly think you can handle another relationship?

JOSHUA:

I don't know, but I know I don't want her to walk away from my life... not now... truthfully not ever.

(ZANE enters)

ZANE:

Joshua just the man I was looking for. I saw your girl Honey Brown last night.

JOSHUA:

Oh shit! That's right she did leave me a message.

LUCIANO:

Now that's the girl you need. My palms are itching just by the thought of her.

(employees enter and begin setting up for business)

JOSHUA:

Man shut up. Wasn't she at Club Paradise?

ZANE:

Yeah, she told me to tell you that she was going to drop by tonight.
She said she missed her big daddy. I don't know why she's lying on
you like that, but anyways Joshua can I borrow five thousand dollars?
I promise I will pay you back with interest.

JOSHUA:

Nigga say what!

ZANE:

Please Joshua please! I'm trying to upgrade my hustle to iPhones and
Samsung Galaxy phones. A friend of mine in New York just came up
on lick. Him and his boys hit a freight down at the New York harbor,
and they are cutting me in on a hellafied deal!

JOSHUA:

Oh, and all you need is five thousand of my money huh?

ZANE:

I already invested three hundred of my own money.

JOSHUA:

Wow!

ZANE:

Joshua please man, I need this by tonight. I'm leaving for New York
in the morning. Please Joshua, I promise I will give you all your
money back and then some.

THE BLACK WIDOW by Charles Bennett

JOSHUA:

(pauses) Man are you sure about this, but them phones are a good ass hustle. I want my money back and some free phones motherfucker!

ZANE:

OK man! I'll give you two of each.

JOSHUA:

OK cool, I will have to write you a check though.

ZANE:

What! Man I ain't got no damn checking account!

JOSHUA:

I know yo' Black ass don't!

I don't even keep my money in the banks. I only deal with the banks far as my business concerns, but never will they have all my money. I just don't trust the banking system. I keep all my money stashed at one of the houses I own, and some with my attorney. I do have some emergency cash here in my safe. Hold on, I'll be right back.

(JOSHUA heads to his office as HONEY enters)

HONEY:

Hello Luciano.

LUCIANO:

Hey, how are you doing Ms. Honey Brown. Are you looking for Joshua?

HONEY:

Yeah, is he here by any chance. Hello Z!

JOSHUA:

(Coming from his office)

OK Z! You better keep your promise.

(startled to see HONEY)

Oh hey Honey. Sorry I didn't call you but....

(HONEY cuts him off)

HONEY:

But you were going to. Uh hmm. (Coolly) Well hello Mr. Joshua.

JOSHUA:

Let's go over here so we can talk.

(they sit at a table)

ZANE:

(talking to LUCIANO)

What do you think he is going to do?

LUCIANO:

Who knows. All I know is that he has been avoiding a lot of phone calls and he is getting too caught up with that chick Rose. Well I gotta go to my office and put in these orders and take care of some business.

(JOSHUA and HONEY talking at a table)

JOSHUA:

Hey Honey, I'm so glad you came by. I need to talk to you about something.

HONEY:

Good because I have some great news to talk about. Go ahead, tell me what you wanted to talk about first.

JOSHUA:

No, let me hear your news first. What you got going on that's so great girl?

HONEY:

OK... OK, I'm so pumped! When I was in Chicago, a talent agent was at our performance and approached me. Josh, this dude has been following me on Instagram and on my YouTube page. I'm not going to sit here and name drop, but he has bigtime successful clients he represents. He has already booked me for events and auditions for some reality shows in L.A.

JOSHUA:

When are you leaving?

HONEY:

Tomorrow morning. Josh, I don't know how long I'm going to be gone. What I am saying is… please Josh, don't be mad at me.

JOSHUA:

Girl are you crazy! I knew this day would come. You are hella talented and ambitious. Whenever I used to stare into your eyes, I could see you looking past me. Looking for that next great adventure. I am so proud of you girl.

HONEY:

Thank you Josh, I knew you would understand. I will always keep in touch, and you know you can always come down and visit and kick it wit yo' girl. Ahh, I'm gone miss you Josh. Just don't hurry up and get married on me soon as I leave. So what was your news?

JOSHUA:

Girl, I totally forgot now.

HONEY:

I'm sure it was something to do with Luciano wondering when I'm going to come back and perform. We all know Luciano is about them dollars!

JOSHUA:

You are probably right.

(both laughing)

HONEY:

Well Joshua, I have to get to my apartment and finish packing for tomorrow's flight.

JOSHUA:

Do you need help moving anything?

HONEY:

My agent is going to handle all my moving arrangements.

JOSHUA:

Well look who's all bigtime already. Well, I guess this is it.

(JOSHUA reaches out to HONEY for a hug goodbye.)

Don't forget me when you become a superstar lil nucca!

(LILY enters the Phat Kat)

LILY:

Z! You seen my cousin Rose? She told me she would be here. We were suppose to go shopping.

ZANE:

Naw, I haven't seen her. Hey would you like to buy a CD? Come with me and checkout my movies. I gotta bunch of new shit in my car. Today, I will give you a good ass deal. Come on with me!

(Gets up and grabs LILY's arm trying to get her to leave)

LILY:

Isn't that Joshua and some chick. Oh hell naw, I knew he wasn't about shit.

(LILY slyly slips out her cellphone and starts recording as HONEY leans closer to JOSHUA)

(ZANE behind her, closer to the door, trying to get LILY to turn around and stop watching HONEY and JOSHUA)

HONEY:

Can I get at least one kiss goodbye Joshua?

(they embrace)

Take care Joshua, I'll miss you, boo.

(HONEY leaves the Phat Kat)

LILY:

That's one of his bitches. I told my cousin he wasn't shit. No good dog!

(LILY finishes recording and slips her phone back in her pocket. ZANE isn't aware of what LILY has done)

Got yo' ass Joshua!

THE BLACK WIDOW by Charles Bennett

LUCIANO:

Come on girl, I got a blunt in my ride too.

> (grabs LILY and pushes her out the door. JOSHUA walks up
> to the bar)

So what does kissing money goodbye feels like?

JOSHUA:

I swear, yo' ass.

LUCIANO:

So did you tell Honey about Rose, because it didn't seem like it.

JOSHUA:

Naw, she was so excited about getting an agent and moving to LA.
She came here to tell me goodbye.

LUCIANO:

She's moving to LA. Damn, money gone. Why didn't you tell her
about Rose?

JOSHUA:

What would be the point? This way, everybody walks away happy
without any drama and nothing can come back to haunt me.

> (ZANE returns to the Phat Kat)

THE BLACK WIDOW by Charles Bennett

ZANE:

Man, you almost got caught up! Lily saw you with Ms. Honey Brown and was tripping. I took her outside and luckily I saw my boy on the corner. I bought her a bag of weed to distract her ass. Man you are playing it close!

JOSHUA:

Man she can do whatever, Honey is moving and now I can fully commit to Rose.

ZANE:

You really like her, don't you?

JOSHUA:

Z, she read me a poem about her feelings. I wanted to play it cool, but now I'm putting caution to the wind and seeing this through.

ZANE:

Are you falling in love with her?

JOSHUA:

I know I don't want to lose her. She's not materialistic, she has a college degree, and she loves children. We were at the park and she started pushing this little boy on the swing. She even held this little girl until her mom came because she fell and bumped her knee and starting crying. Rose held her and started crying too and man it touched me. She's a beautiful woman inside and out.

THE BLACK WIDOW by Charles Bennett

ZANE:

Josh you are sounding like a little bitch right about now.

(both start laughing)

Fo' real man, she has all the qualities that a woman should have. Z, I could see myself being happy with just her and her alone. That's why I'm glad Honey is moving so I can be with just Rose!

ZANE:

Josh, since you are going full bitch, I guess I can join in.

On the real Josh the main reason I am going to New York is to try to get my life back. I miss my daughter and Angela. I never told you why Angela and I broke up. I was trying to be a rapper and I brought Angela to New York with me to make it big. Man we struggled, but over time Angela got pregnant. Label after label wasn't feeling me and I went to a state of depression. I couldn't afford Pampers, Similac, baby wipes... nothing! I decided to head out to Cali and try my luck. Times got so hard I started grinding.

JOSHUA:

You started selling dope?

ZANE:

Yeah, I lied about the money I sent to Angela. I told her that my label gave me an advance, but I was giving her drug money.

JOSHUA:

Damn Z.

ZANE:

Yeah, it gets worse. I got caught and did two years in jail. In jail all I did was think about them.

JOSHUA:

That's your family!

ZANE:

Yeah! Angela and my baby girl Keisha. I truly missed her, seeing her laugh and getting sick. Man those were the best times. When she got sick, I would get her out her crib and we would lay on the couch and sleep together. I would listen to her snore like her mother. She would rest her elbows on my chest waiting for me to wake up. Just like her mother would do. She even turned her head sideways and give me this dumb look......just like her momma. Man I miss the hell out of them, but mainly I miss my little angel Keisha. Angela and I aren't promised to be together always, but Keisha will always be mine. When I look at her, I remember all the love that Angela and I had for each other when we made her. She will always represent true love. I have to reconnect with my daughter before it's too late.

JOSHUA:

Z, you are starting to sound like a lil-bitch right about now.

(they both start laughing. JOSHUA reaches into his pocket and gives ZANE the money with an extra five hundred dollars)

ZANE:

Josh hold up, that's more than I asked you for.

JOSHUA:

This is for you to buy Keisha something real pretty. No matter what, buy Angela some flowers and take your family out to dinner. Food is always good for the soul.

ZANE:

Josh are you trying to hint to me that you are hungry?

JOSHUA:

Hell yeah!

ZANE:

Let me buy you something to eat, wit' yo' money.

(they exit the bar together)

(lights black out)

ACT 5
SCENE 2

(Later that day. LILY and ROSE enter the bar)

ROSE:

So where is he?

LILY:

I'm telling you he was here kissing up on this chick. She's probably one of his many hoes. See look at my phone. I think it's that Eryka Badu bitch.

ROSE:

I can't believe his ass. I just told him how much he meant to me and in a matter of seconds he's kissing some broad!

LILY:

I told you what you need to do. Girl, you know where we are from. It's time Joshua learned about the dirty South. It's time he got introduced to voodoo. That will teach his ass a lesson. Grandma said this spell will make him love you forever and his soul will never find any rest until he is with his true love. No woman will ever arouse him again. He will only have sexual desires for his true love.

ROSE:

Girl, I don't know if I want to take it that far.

LILY:

That far! He probably left here with her to get some pussy. He doesn't deserve you or any other woman. Do it girl!

ROSE:

(reluctant) Will it last forever?

LILY:

What! I know you ain't changing your mind. Don't nobody fucks over my family. Oh hell no! I will just do it myself!

ROSE:

No! I will do it, but we can break the spell whenever we want right?

LILY:

Yeah whatever!

ROSE:

Seriously Lily!

LILY:

Yeah! Do you remember what you have to do?

ROSE:

Yes. I make him the drink with the ingredients of the spell. After he drinks it, I will make love to him. How will I be able to say the chant without him getting suspicious?

LILY:

I don't know. Use your creativity. If you are changing your mind, I
have no problem doing it myself Rose. The moon is in the right phase
to cast this spell. It's now or never. The hell with you, I will do it
myself!

ROSE:

No! If anybody is going to do it, it should be me.

LILY:

OK, make sure he drinks it all. That way the spell will work for sure.
Then Mr. Joshua will never get the chance to use his little thing on
nobody else. The only time he will make love will be in his dreams
and the only woman he will dream about is you. Every night this will
continue to happen over and over again.

ROSE:

Until we break it.

LILY:

Yeah, he will learn never to mess with us!

(lights black out)

ACT 6
SCENE 1

(The lights come up with the Phat Kat staff cleaning.
LUCIANO and JOSHUA are behind the bar)

LUCIANO:

So I see your girl Rose didn't show up tonight.

JOSHUA:

Yeah, I'm tripping about that myself.

LUCIANO:

Well there's your girl right now.

(he comes around from the bar to talk with the staff)
OK everybody lets go home for tonight. I see you tomorrow Joshua.

(LUCIANO exits the bar along with the staff)

JOSHUA:

I am glad you came by Rose.

ROSE:

Is that so!

JOSHUA:

Yeah, I wanted to see you!

ROSE:

I bet! Go sit on the couch, I want to make you a special drink to get you in the mood and show you how much I appreciate you waiting for me.

> (JOSHUA, looking shocked, walks over to the couch center stage. ROSE goes to the bar and prepares the drink, slipping in the voodoo ingredients where JOSHUA can't see)

I really hope that me playing hard to get wasn't a turn off. I would hate to think that I jeopardized the good thing we have.

JOSHUA:

I was never turned off. Honestly I….

ROSE:

(ROSE cuts him off)

I know you can make the ladies feel good Josh. Don't you want to make me feel good?

JOSHUA

I want to make you feel good, but I really want for you to feel special.

ROSE:

(sarcastic) You want me to feel special. Oh you are such a smooth talker. I bet you tell all the ladies that Joshua.

JOSHUA:

(pulling ROSE close to him)

In the past few years, no I haven't. Yeah Rose, I can make you feel good. I can make you have orgasm after orgasm. Then what happens after that Rose? I want more than just to make you feel good. I want you to come to me always. When you are sad, hurt, and depress. I want you to come to me when you have dreams and ambitions. When you are full of ideas and nobody wants to listen. I want you to come to me. Feeling good is temporary, but feeling special. Rose, I'll give you that forever and I mean that always.

(they start kissing but ROSE is having second thoughts)

ROSE:

(stops kissing to look Joshua in his eyes)

Just promise me to be honest and always truthful Josh. Never keep secrets and never tell me lies.

JOSHUA:

Always Rose.

ROSE:

(contemplating should she still go along with the voodoo)

Is there anything I should know about Joshua? Any lies or secrets you are keeping from me right now?

JOSHUA:

(thinking about HONEY, not knowing ROSE has seen the video clip of them kissing)

No Rose, I have no secrets.

ROSE:

(convinced to go ahead with the voodoo spell, ROSE walks
backs to get the drink mixed with the voodoo potion and
returns with it to JOSHUA)

Just relax and drink this.

JOSHUA:

(drinking) Hmmm this tastes good! What kind of drink is this?

ROSE:

A make you feel good drink. Make sure you drink it all, I want you to
get your buzz on.

(ROSE slowly undresses herself down to her lingerie)

JOSHUA:

Oh!

(making himself more relaxed on the couch)

ROSE:

Oh! You will see.

(sitting on JOSHUA's lap)

Joshua do you want me?

JOSHUA:

Yes Rose, I want you.

THE BLACK WIDOW by Charles Bennett

ROSE:

Joshua do you promise?

JOSHUA:

Yes!

ROSE:

You must make me a promise. A solemn swear that you will always want me even when you are sleep.

JOSHUA:

Yes Rose.

ROSE:

You will never desire another woman. You will only desire me.

JOSHUA:

Yes Rose.

ROSE:

Say it.

JOSHUA:

I will never desire another woman. I will always want you day and night, and even in my dreams.

ROSE:

So be it Joshua. So be it.

(begins kissing his neck and moves closer to his ear)

JOSHUA:

What are you whispering in my ear? Is that Spanish?

ROSE:

Only how much you mean to me. You so damn sexy, you got me speaking in tongues. Joshua do you still want me?

JOSHUA:

Yes Rose, I want you.

(they begin kissing)

ROSE:

Do you love me?

JOSHUA:

Yes Rose. I love you.

ROSE:

Good! That's all I needed to hear.

(music begins playing)

(blackout and segue into next scene)

THE BLACK WIDOW by Charles Bennett

ACT 7
SCENE 1

(lights remain down, the voice of JOSHUA will read a poem in the blackout)

Some months has passed,

since I enjoyed a good laugh.

Then I remember,

you made me that drink

Yo' body and words along with your seduce.

You were in my ear singing that strange tune.

I should've known.

I should've knew.

That you,

You knew voodoo.

I remember you wanting me to make a promise, a solemn swear.

I was shy, I was scared.

But your body was so lovely,

I couldn't resist, I gave in to your dare.

Now I realize I was a fool!

That was part of your trap.

THE BLACK WIDOW by Charles Bennett

That was your voodoo!

(lights black out)

ACT 7
SCENE 2

(The lights come up with the bar fully crowded.
TERRANCE is talking to Luciano who is behind the bar)

TERRANCE:

Please tell me she is coming? This girl is hot! In Chicago she put the mic to a blaze. The girl is fire! You hear me Luciano... Fire!

LUCIANO:

She was to do me a favor first, and she said she would come here after she checked on Joshua for me.

TERRANCE:

I just want to make sure I got Ms. Honey Brown coming. I'm nervous as hell! OK, Reggie is here, and you are reading. Let me calm down because I plan on reading myself.

LUCIANO:

Will you please relax Terrance. Just go up there and get tonight started. Honey just text me, and she will be hear any minute.

TERRANCE:

It's showtime!

(TERRANCE walks onto the stage)

Good evening ladies and gentlemen. I welcome you to poetry night at the Phat Kat lounge. I will be your host for tonight. My name is Terrance.

(HONEY walks in and goes to the bar by LUCIANO.)

Before I even get started, we have Ms. Honey Brown in the house y'all! Please show some love for Ms. Honey Brown! Tonight is a night for dedications. I will like to start this evening by reading a poem dedicated to my first love. Even though I broke her heart, I still regret walking away from her. I know some of y'all are saying, "aren't you a homosexual"? The truth is, I'm a bisexual. I love men and women, but I'm still single. Ain't that a bitch! You would think by me having both options, I would be happily in love. Well I'm not. I figured by coming out the closet and being true to myself I would find love, but I'm still confused then as I am now. I just knew she wouldn't accept me, if she knew I was a bisexual. People think being bi is all about having threesomes and wild orgies. Hell, it could be! I'm still waiting for my invitations.

(laughs) Anyways, this poem is dedicated to my first love. It's called "My System."

I'm trying so hard

I'm trying so hard

I'm trying not to listen

To that voice inside of me

Saying she would never accept yo' style of living

I'm trying to turn away

From all this pain

But in the back of my mind

THE BLACK WIDOW by Charles Bennett

I know I want to stay

Just to say

Just to say

I just can't

I just can't

Get you out of my system

And every slow song that I hear

Always got my missing

Your love, yo' touch

Right now oh girl I need it so much

Yo' face, yo' hair

How I wish my hands were right there

But no, I gotta let you go

But I got these songs just blazing in my stereo

I'm going to lose control

So I turn down the volume

And listen to this song

Go deeper and deeper

Into my soul

THE BLACK WIDOW by Charles Bennett

The more I listen, I begin to think

The more I think, I get weak

I been playing this same song

For too long

I'm like a fiend, fiending for a hit

I'm like a prostitute who continues

To be used and abused because she's

So damn in love with her pimp

My pride is telling me to pull out the CD

And throw it to the floor

But every time I do, I just pick it right back up

And play it some mo'!

I gotta get you out of my system

But my heart loves this song

So that's why I keep listening

And the way we use to dance

It was like sheer romance

See ya'll, ya'll don't understand

This was once our song when I was her man

THE BLACK WIDOW by Charles Bennett

I gotta face the deal

She doesn't love me anymore

And that's shit real

It's time for me to heal, resume

And stop playing this song that makes me feel so blue

I gotta get in check

Protect what's left of my heart

And stop holding on to all these regrets

So I push eject!

But I can't

I can't

Get you out of my system

And every slow song that I hear

Always got me missing

You!

TERRANCE:

We gone keep this party going. The next poet we have coming up tonight, is the co-owner of the Phat Kat. The one and only Luciano!

(Walks off the stage clapping towards LUCIANO.)

THE BLACK WIDOW by Charles Bennett

LUCIANO:

This is going to be a little different for me tonight. This poem is
dedicated to my ex-wife. Can y'all believe that? The woman I call a
money pit, I am actually dedicating a poem to? Truthfully, it's long
overdue. I may complain about her, but we took vows together. I
meant those vows, but I didn't honor those vows. Anyways, before I
get all Drake on y'all, let me just read the poem. This poem is titled,
"If I Can't Have Forever."

I know deep down it could never be.

This vision I have of you and me,

but girl I'm gone keep on wishing

and hope your heart will listen

because it's you right now I'm missing.

So your pictures I'm gone keep on kissing.

If I can't have forever

Then I'll just take whatever.

Whatever you want from me.

Whatever you feel the need

To call on me baby.

I can wait this time.

Whatever it takes to make you mine

Cause damn I need you in my life,

but my ways are so damn trife

So I'm just gone pray for whatever.

To get us back together,

but I know it won't be right

So that's why I fight

With all my might

When I see you in my sight…to say

Girl I'm gone keep on wishing

and your pictures I'm gone keep on kissing,

because it's you right now I'm missing

because it's you right now I'm missing

Girl I'm gone keep on wishing

and your pictures I'm gone keep on kissing,

because it's you right now I'm missing

because it's you right now I'm missing

If I can't have forever

Then I'll just take whatever

Whatever you want from me

THE BLACK WIDOW by Charles Bennett

Whenever you want to be pleased

Girl, I'll drop to my knees

To plead

Baby just be with me

I know this thought is like whatever,

but damn I wanted this forever!

For all the time I breathe

That you would be here with me,

but I know this ain't reality.

So I'll just cherish our memories

We've been apart for too long,

but my feelings for you are still strong.

Shit, you the reason why I wrote this poem,

but it's time that I moved on.

Am I wrong,

Am I wrong,

I know damn well, I was wrong.

Because when I had you

I didn't think forever.

THE BLACK WIDOW by Charles Bennett

I treated you just like whatever.

Whenever I had the time

and now you are forever on my mind.

Our situation will never get better,

but I really wanted us to be forever

and ever

and ever

but whatever.

Girl I'm gone keep on wishing

and your pictures I'm gone keep on kissing

because it's you right now I'm missing

because it's you right now I'm missing.

Girl I'm gone keep on wishing

and your pictures I'm gone keep on kissing

because it's you right now I'm missing

because it's you right now I'm missing

Forever!

TERRANCE:

Ohhh, somebody still in love. Did he say forever ever! I think you need to call your ex-wife. I think she would love to hear that, what

THE BLACK WIDOW by Charles Bennett

y'all think? That was beautiful, and from the soul. Admit you was wrong nucca! (laughs) OK y'all, once again give it up to Luciano. The next poet we have coming to the stage is Reggie, but he prefers to be called Chocolate Thunder… boy bye!

(walks off the stage laughing)

REGGIE:

That's right y'all! Chocolate Thunder is in the building. Ain't nothing like the taste of Chocolate. How y'all doing tonight? My poem is a dedication to a woman whose name is sweet as honey. I have seen this woman here and there, and each time has been as breathtaking as the first. This poem I have for y'all tonight is called, "Baby, You Got a Fan."

The few times I have seen you

Your presence was from afar,

but your beauty shines like a burning star.

I will probably never have the nerve to speak,

but please do not worry

I am not some psychotic freak.

For I do not want you to feel at danger

Or think your life is in harm.

I just want to tell you how beautiful you are.

Once I imagined you were made of ice cream,

THE BLACK WIDOW by Charles Bennett

and you were outside on a hot sunny day.

As the minutes passed

You were slowly melting away.

As I stood there too shy to face you eye to eye.

I was like a simple man and stayed behind.

My tongue lust to lick the drop

That was running down to the arch of your spine.

Then I close my eyes,

and began to fantasize.

My tongue was now the sun,

and your body remained ice cream.

As my tongue licked every part of your body.

You had no choice but to melt

Inside of me.

As I licked my lips

Imagining the flavor of your cream.

I notice you felt my stare

and turned to see,

but your eyes sparkles like diamonds

THE BLACK WIDOW by Charles Bennett

and I realized for me to stare

would only have me trapped

forever in your beauty.

Your eyes sit in your face

Like two beautiful gems.

Any man who looks at you

Can be lured and will never be the same again.

For this has happen in my case

Because I still remember the mole

On the left side of your face.

Shiiidd, I could be wrong

It was probably your right,

but when I saw you at the jewelry stand

none of those shiny stones

could compare to your eyes.

There is one thing

I want you to understand.

I know deep down inside

I could never be your man,

THE BLACK WIDOW by Charles Bennett

but I want you to know

here in Cleveland Heights!

Baby, you got a fan!

TERRANCE:

Uhh hmm! Honey Brown, don't you have a mole on the left side of your face? I think you have a secret admirer Ms. Honey, and speaking on that note... The moment you all have been waiting for. Ya'll know her as Ms. Honey Brown from the group Shades Of Essence. The poetry group, slash singing group, slash acting crew. We have Ms. Honey Brown for your feature poet for tonight.

HONEY:

Hello everybody! Greetings and blessings to all. I just want to say to Mr. Reggie, thank you for the poem. I was truly flattered and impressed. What y'all think! Honey and melted chocolate together? Hmm. (smiling and laughing) I'm so glad y'all came out tonight. This poem I have tonight is for my Nubian Queens. This poem is a dedication and tribute to my sisters. It's a celebration to the love and joy we bring to this world, and how any man is blessed to be in our presence. There is no king without a queen, but dammit you gone respect me. Ain't that right my sisters! Tonight, I honor us in this poem. The poem is called, "Essence."

Black woman,

when he made you.

He should have made you a fragrance.

THE BLACK WIDOW by Charles Bennett

Because once he gets a whiff of you,

you control his essence.

The way your skin color sinuates your clothes.

Oh the many things he would do to

you if ya'll were alone.

How could we go through time

not knowing we are so damn fine?

Don't perm it out,

or thin it out.

He loves the way we are

no doubt!

Our full lips,

our big ole hips,

black women!

We are truly magnificent!

I got to give it up to you.

For remaining strong,

and doing the things that you do.

When we pass him by

THE BLACK WIDOW by Charles Bennett

he's too much of a punk to say hi.

He loves the way we slide.

We are going to stay fine

until the day we die.

He tries to fight this feeling.

You know men,

they got too much pride.

But he loses all courage

once he gazes into our eyes.

No other woman has made them

feel this way.

No other woman has been

a better game.

They say the blacker the berry

the sweeter the juice.

Shit, they love us in all

Shades from dark and lovely

To the red bones too.

We are so sexy,

THE BLACK WIDOW by Charles Bennett

Sisters stand up

Let the world see us shine!

From a scale through

One to ten.

Our figure is too astronomical for him

To calculate in his mind.

Let him fall into our love.

Only we can make living down here

Feel like heaven above.

With us, he has faith.

Our beauty is the closest thing

To compare to an angel's face.

Black women.

When I think of us,

I think of elegance.

Once a man absorbs us.

We become his essence.

HONEY:

Thank you people. Thank you.

THE BLACK WIDOW by Charles Bennett

(TERRANCE walks back to the stage)

TERRANCE:

Give it up to Ms. Honey Brown. People, give it up! Thank you girl for coming tonight. Thank you. Well everybody that's going to put this night to a close. I hope you enjoyed yo'selves and please come back to the Phat Kat again. And please give it up one more time for Ms. Honey Brown.

(TERRANCE goes and talks to his group of friends as HONEY goes over to talk to Luciano.)

HONEY:

I did what you asked me. I stopped by his house and man was it a mess. He was asleep when I stopped by, and his breath was straight liquor. He was glad to see me, and he washed up a little and straighten up his place but it wasn't the same Joshua I once knew. Out of pity, I seduced and teased him like old times. We started making out and suddenly he stopped. He started saying, "oh you still won't let me! I get it." Then he told me this crazy story that someone put a voodoo spell on him. He said that he only dreams about this one girl night after night. When he tries to think about other women his dick don't work. He started shouting, "that damn bitch put a spell on me!" Then he called her a Black Widow and grabbed pen and paper and went into his bedroom. I decided to stay and clean his place up while he was writing. That's what took me so long to get here.

LUCIANO:

Yeah he's been like this for the past few months. It's getting worse day by day.

THE BLACK WIDOW by Charles Bennett

(ZANE enters the bar)

ZANE:

My main man Linguini! What's up homie? Did you miss me!

LUCIANO:

Well if it ain't crazy ass Z! Mr. Walmart, Mr. Best Buy, Mr. Hook-up man!

ZANE:

(Looking at TERRANCE talking to HONEY)

Where's Joshua?

HONEY:

(Walks back to the bar to talk to LUCIANO)

Well Luciano, I'm going to get out of here. Your boy Terrance here has invited me to hang out with him and his buddies. I don't have nothing else to do and he seems pretty cool. Take care Luciano. I wish you guys the best.

(HONEY walks back over to TERRANCE and his friends.)

ZANE:

What's up Luciano! Where's Joshua?

(ZANE reaches into his pocket and drops a stack of bills on the bar.)

For all my homies. Drinks are on me!

LUCIANO:

Wow! What gives?

ZANE:

Man, I went to New York and my connection got arrested. I was so depressed that I needed a good laugh. I went to a comedy club and they had open mic night. Well, I decided to go up there and tell the story of my life, and ended up winning six hundred dollars. So I kept going to comedy clubs and winning contest after contest, and bam baby I'm a star! I have an agent now, and I'm making good money as a local talent in New York. I came back to give Joshua his money. His money made it possible for me to stay afloat while I was staying in New York. He allowed me to get my second chance at life. That's my dog! By the way, what's up with the gay guy being the host for poetry night?

LUCIANO:

You mean Terrance. Well Joshua hasn't been hosting poetry night anymore, and Terrance and his buddies kept coming back waiting for the next poetry night to happen. So I decided to let Terrance be the guest host for poetry night until Josh comes back. So you're a big time comedian now?

ZANE:

Yeah, I'm rich bitch! Why did JOSHUA stop hosting poetry night?

LUCIANO:

A lot has changed since you left Z.

(REGGIE comes over.)

REGGIE:

What's up Z! So you finally came back to Cleveland huh!

ZANE:

Yeah man, I'm back in the land!

REGGIE:

Z, I would love to catch up with you, but Terrance has invited me to hang out with him and Honey Brown tonight. As you can see, Terrance got some of his lesbian friends with him so I will catch up with you later pimpin'.

ZANE:

I thought you were in love with Honey Brown?

REGGIE:

Hey! If Honey is on some bullshit, maybe I can bring one of them lesbians back to the darkside. (starts laughing and begins to leave) I'll check y'all out later.

ZANE:

So what did you mean a lot has changed? What's the deal with Joshua? Is there something you not telling me? What's up with Joshua... tell me!

THE BLACK WIDOW by Charles Bennett

LUCIANO:

I believe he's gone crazy Z. Joshua believes that Lily's cousin put a voodoo spell on him. This spell has him only dreaming about her every night and with other women his dick won't get hard. He's looking bad and talking crazy Z. I got in touch with Honey to see if she could help him, but it didn't work.

ZANE:

Oh my God! Joshua is not making this up. I told him to leave them Louisiana women alone, I bet Lily had something to do with this.

LUCIANO:

Why would you say that?

ZANE:

The night I asked Joshua for the money, Lily came by looking for her cousin. I dragged Lily out of here so Joshua could talk to Honey in peace. I came back and told him, but he said Honey was moving and he was going to commit to Rose. There was nothing to worry about.

LUCIANO:

Yeah Z, I thought the same thing. She came by that same night and I thought everything was going to be cool.

ZANE:

So what happen after that?

LUCIANO:

At first he was normal, but by the next month he was acting strange. He started talking about the same dream he kept on having night after night about Rose. Then Joshua started acting crazy.

ZANE:

Man it's my fault, I should've done something.

LUCIANO:

Z, there was nothing you could have done.

ZANE:

I got to make this right. Is Joshua's number still the same?

LUCIANO:

Yeah, but he doesn't answer his phone anymore.

ZANE:

That's alright; I will just text him.

(ZANE heads for the store)

LUCIANO:

Where are you going?

ZANE:

To find Lily! If she's still a weed-head, I know where I can find her.

LUCIANO:

Z, there's nothing you can do.

(ZANE writes hastily on a piece of paper)

ZANE:

I wouldn't have gotten to New York if it wasn't for Josh. I have to try something. If they get here before I get back give Lily this letter. I gotta go save my boy.

(ZANE exits)

(lights black out)

ACT 7
SCENE 3

(the lights come on. The bar is empty except for TIFFANY cleaning the bar. LILY enters)

LILY:

Hello is Zane here?

TIFFANY:

No, but he told me to give you this note if you got here before he did.

LILY:

(reads the letter out loud)

"Lily if you and your cousin get here before I get back please wait for me. Please Lily don't let me down." I wonder what this is all about?

(LILY grabs her cellphone and makes a call.)

Rose are you almost here yet? Who? (starts laughing) Naw, Joshua is not here. OK girl hurry up! (hangs up the cell and talks to herself) He better give me some weed for this.

(ZANE enters)

ZANE:

Lily, I'm glad you came. Where's your cousin Rose?

LILY:

I just called her. Hold your horses boy! First tell me where you've been and what you've been up to. Also, you still smoking?

ZANE:

Same ole Lily. Well I live in New York now working as a comedian, can you believe that? Now I get paid for talking shit. As for smoking no! That shit clouds your mind and makes you think crazy thoughts.

LILY:

Oh it's like that Z!

TIFFANY:

Z, Luciano told me to give you Joshua's old keys to the bar because Joshua has another set of keys with him. So when you leave just lock the bar up.

(TIFFANY hands ZANE the keys and leaves the bar.)

ZANE:

Lily let me get right down to the point. You and your cousin has caused my boy a lot of grief.

LILY:

No! Your boy brought that to himself. I saw with my own two eyes Joshua kissing that girl and Zane you were there so don't try to start no shit!

(ROSE enters the bar.)

ZANE:

No Lily, what you saw was Joshua saying goodbye to that girl because he wanted your cousin.

THE BLACK WIDOW by Charles Bennett

LILY:

Whatever Z!

ZANE:

(looking at ROSE) Joshua knew that he was falling in love with you Rose. He was only kissing Honey goodbye. He said that he was going to commit to you Rose and only you.

LILY:

What does this has to do with me?

ROSE:

Everything Lily! This has everything to do with you.

LILY:

Rose, his ass is lying! He's trying to defend his boy.

ZANE:

Yo' weed smoking jealous ass was always upset that Joshua was talking to your cousin. The night you decided not to come to poetry night because you wanted to get high started the love connection between Rose and Joshua. Yo' ass started hating Joshua ever since.

ROSE:

Lily is this true? Did you make me do that because deep down inside you were mad at Joshua? Huh Lily, were you mad because he wanted me?

ZANE:

You damn right she was mad, because of her, a man is living his life in misery.

LILY:

Dammit! He deserved it!

ZANE:

Why Lily, because he wanted your cousin and not you? All the time you invested in here, and night after night you came to see Joshua and he had the nerve to overlook you! You were his number one fan, but he choose your cousin instead of you!

LILY:

Hell yes! How could he! He knew damn well I wanted him and he decided to date my cousin! Could you imagine the shame I suffered? How stupid he made me look! Yes, I hated Joshua!

ZANE:

Enough to put a voodoo spell on him, right?

(LILY and ROSE look at each other. After a long moment of silence ROSE speaks)

ROSE:

Yes Z! There was enough hate to put a spell on Joshua. (starts crying) Why Lily? Why didn't you tell me that you didn't want me to date Joshua?

THE BLACK WIDOW by Charles Bennett

LILY:

You always get what you want Rose. You always gotten the better things in life. Joshua was mine, and you took him away from me.

ROSE:

He was never yours, that's what you told me. I loved him Lily, and I still do!

LILY:

Maybe we can make a spell and make another Joshua if that will make you happy.

ROSE:

Shut up you cold hearted bitch! How could you Lily? Lily find a way to break the spell!

LILY:

No!

ROSE:

Dammit Lily, I'm not asking you I'm telling you! Break the damn spell!

LILY:

No! Because I can't.

ROSE:

What?

THE BLACK WIDOW by Charles Bennett

LILY:

You heard me, I can't.

ZANE:

Come on Lily, is it because you don't want to?

LILY:

No! The spell cannot be broken.

ROSE:

(runs to LILY in rage and grabs her.)

You said we could break it anytime we wanted. Lily, you said we could break it whenever!

(all lights out except a spot on LILY)

LILY:

I lied.

(back to normal lighting)

ZANE:

(talking directly to ROSE)

Anything can be broken Rose. Don't believe your cousin. She's full of lies. Who do you think would know how to break this spell?

ROSE:

If anybody would know it would be our grandmother.

THE BLACK WIDOW by Charles Bennett

ZANE:

Rose, I don't know how you feel about Joshua now but if you have any compassion stop this madness now!

ROSE:

I will Z, I will.

(starts to leave but turns back to talk to Z.)

Z, tell Joshua I'm sorry. I hate what I've done because I never once stopped loving him. I know this may sound crazy, but I thought after it happen Joshua would fall madly in love with me and would come looking for me. He never did, but I was always waiting for him... always.

(ROSE leaves.)

LILY:

Poor little Rose.

ZANE:

What is your problem Lily?

LILY:

You know it was my mother's idea to name Rose and I after flowers, but people always pass the lilies and go straight to the roses. Well I'm tired of being overlooked and forgotten. That's why I wanted someone else to feel my pain.

ZANE:

Joshua?

LILY:

(with increasing emotion) I loved him more than Rose ever could have, and if he didn't want my love... the hell with him!

ZANE:

No Lily! The hell with you.

(ZANE walks into JOSHUA's office. LILY shouts after him)

LILY:

He deserves it! The son of a bitch should of love me, not her... me!

(lights black out)

ACT 7
SCENE 4

(JOSHUA enters the Phat Kat and goes behind the bar.
There are no customers or staff present. He makes himself a
drink, and walks to the stage.)

JOSHUA:

(sips his drink. He looks weary and maybe drunk)

Oh yeah that good ole 151. Ladies and gentleman how the hell are
ya'll feeling tonight in the Phat Kat. Where we always keep it Phat
for ya'll.

(laughs, sips) Oh yeah, this shit will put some hair on yo' chest. Once
again poetry people, what it is? How do ya'll live? Who me, oh I'm
just living like every day is Thanksgiving! Except some chick got a
doll of me with pins in my dick! (laughing)

(ZANE comes out of JOSHUA's office and sees JOSHUA
on the stage.)

Z! What's up man! Come holla at yo' boy!

ZANE:

Joshua! Man I need to talk to you big time.

JOSHUA:

Talk to me baby.

ZANE:

Joshua everything is going to be alright. You were right! You do have
a voodoo spell on you, but I talked to Rose. Joshua she's sorry for
what she's done. Lily put that crazy idea in her head. She wants to
break the spell. Joshua please stop drinking and listen to what I am
telling you…

(JOSHUA cuts him off)

JOSHUA:

Listen for what Zane it's too late. I'm already knocking on heaven's
door.

ZANE:

Joshua she's agreed to break the spell. Man she is sorry and she said
she never stopped loving you.

JOSHUA:

You're right because she's been loving me every night for the past
few months. (singing) If loving you is wrong, I don't wanna be right!

ZANE:

Joshua please stop drinking and listen to me.

JOSHUA:

I will listen to everything you have to say, but first be the only person
tonight to hear my last poem. It's about death. I wrote a poem about
it. You want to hear it? Well here it goes. It's called "The Black
Widow." (getting angry) You like that shit don't you? That's a sweet

title huh? "The Black Widow…" that's because she has killed me! (calms himself down.) Z! Hear my last poem.

(Joshua walks towards the stage.)

ZANE:

Joshua why don't you just listen to me. Rose said she was sorry and at this moment she is learning how to break the spell.

JOSHUA:

(turns around to speak directly to ZANE.)

Oh! So she's cooking up another batch. Ain't this about a bitch. What this one going to do? Rise me from the dead? (loud and angry) Do you smell what the Rose gots cooking… Nigga it's voodoo!

ZANE:

Come on Joshua, chill out man.

JOSHUA:

Listen to my last poem and I will chill.

ZANE:

Joshua whatever you want man. Just relax.

JOSHUA:

OK Z! Listen to this, it's a classic. It's sad, but it's the truth. I realized why Rose put the spell on me. I didn't tell Honey the truth about her and I. I had this coming. Zane listen to my final poem, "The Black Widow."

THE BLACK WIDOW by Charles Bennett

The Black Widow

You ever heard of that saying,

you weep what you sow?

Well I'm living testimony and

here's how my story goes.

See,

I loved a woman,

but truly I don't think she loved me in return.

Due to previous disappointment

she grew bitter

and now her heart

was stone.

We only once made love,

but somehow it was 4-life.

I could see deep in her eyes

The effects of pain, dissent, and lies.

I offered her love,

But love

she grew to despise.

THE BLACK WIDOW by Charles Bennett

She left me a note.

She left it, on my pillow.

It said you just made love.

To, the Black Widow.

She said a man like me

Filled her head with lies

About, one day his last name

she will hold,

and together they would grow old

Well, she grew cold

and vengeance

one day she shall unfold.

Cause now night after night.

You see,

she's, in my dreams.

Loving me,

caressing me,

the way I always wanted

love to be.

THE BLACK WIDOW by Charles Bennett

Now when I walk the streets.

Women in reality don't mean shit to me.

I just wanna go home and sleep,

and be with her in my dreams.

She left me a note.

She left it, on my pillow.

Said you just made love.

To, the Black Widow.

And for now on

and the rest of your life.

You will never have the appetite.

To make any woman your wife.

I killed in you,

the one thing I valued to be so true.

You will only desire for me.

But you can only have me in your dreams.

Day after day,

oh, you will pray.

Wishing I will return.

THE BLACK WIDOW by Charles Bennett

Wishing, I will stay.

And once just like me

you will sit and wait.

And you will wait,

by the window.

Oh what a tangled web we weave.

Signed, the Black Widow.

ZANE:

Joshua it's not like that, she didn't mean it man! She's sorry for all the pain she has caused you.

JOSHUA:

Well Z, you know what! It's too damn late because Elvis is leaving the building!

(walks towards ZANE)

ZANE:

Joshua stop cracking jokes and listen dammit!

JOSHUA:

Z, I'm going crazy man and I had to stop this madness. So I did.

(JOSHUA sits heavily on the couch center-stage.)

ZANE:

What are you talking about?

JOSHUA:

It will be over soon. I will be with Rose forever in my dreams. It's such a beautiful place Z, I'm about to take a long deep sleep.

ZANE:

What are you saying Josh?

JOSHUA:

Man I took some pills and there is no turning back. Say goodbye Z, I'm leaving this world. I want to live in my dreams and so I am.

> (reaches into his pocket and pulls out two empty prescription bottles. ZANE picks them up and reads the labels. ROSE enters the bar.)

ZANE:

Joshua, no you didn't. (pauses) Why did you do this Josh?

> (ZANE sits on the opposite couch with a confused look on his face.)

ROSE:

> (realizes something is wrong by looking at ZANE and runs to JOSHUA.)

JOSHUA!

JOSHUA:

(the pills have started taking effect and JOSHUA is starting to die.)

Rose, the most beautiful flower of them all.....my Rose.

ROSE:

Joshua, I'm so sorry, but everything is going to be alright now. I know how to break the spell. Joshua, it's over. Joshua please forgive me. I love you, I never stopped loving you.

JOSHUA:

Please forgive me Rose. I am so sorry I wasn't honest. I'm going to be with you forever, and I have to make sure you forgive me.

(his breathing becomes less and less)

You are just as beautiful as you are in my dreams. Oh Rose, you so pretty. I will always love you.

(JOSHUA falls to the side and his life slowly fades away)

ROSE:

JOSHUA! No JOSHUA no!

(getting louder each time she says his name)

JOSHUA no! JOSHUA!

(Music begins to play right before the blackout.)

(lights black out)

ACT 8
SCENE 1

(Music is still playing before the lights come up. TERRANCE is on the stage. LUCIANO is behind the bar talking to TIFFANY.)

(Lights come up)

TERRANCE:

Once again, thank you everyone for coming out and sharing your poems with us tonight. Please come back again and bring a friend.

(TERRANCE walks over to the table where his friends are sitting, stage right.)

LUCIANO:

(talking to ZANE)

I know it's poetry night, but it's not the same without Joshua. I truly miss him.

ZANE :

It's a shame it had to be such a rushed funeral.

LUCIANO:

Yeah, but his power of attorney said that Josh specifically said that he did not want his organs touched upon his death. I remember him always saying, "They ain't gone cut me up like they did my parents. Asking if they smoked or diabetics. Knowing damn well it was all about the melanin. Naw, not with me!" So the people at the funeral home said we had to bury his body as soon possible before he started smelling.

ZANE:

Man, Josh know he had some major trust issues. (both laughing) Man, I'm gone miss him.

(They look sadly at each other. ROSE enters the bar.)

ROSE:

Hi Luciano.

LUCIANO:

Hello Rose, is everything OK?

ROSE:

Yeah, I was wondering if it isn't too late could I read a poem tonight? It's for Joshua.

LUCIANO:

Sure Rose.

(LUCIANO flags down TERRANCE and points at ROSE and then points to the stage.)

TERRANCE:

(LUCIANO catches TERRANCE's eye. TERRANCE looks at LUCIANO and ROSE by the stage and nods; he talks to the small crowd.)

Excuse me everyone, but we have one more poet coming to the stage tonight. Please give her a warm welcome.

(ROSE walks to the stage.)

ROSE:

Hello everybody, my name is Rose and I would like to share this poem with ya'll. (takes a deep breath.) Before I read this poem, I would like to say to all the couples out there, cherish the ones you love. Never let your friends or family cloud your judgment or influence you to think negative about the one you love. If you love someone never be afraid to tell them. Love is beautiful. Always remember that. This poem is dedicated to a man I will always love. (pauses for a moment.) This is for you Joshua. It's titled, "What Am I Going To Do?"

I have written my poetry

with a broken heart,

and a face

scarred by bitter tears.

Those poems were special,

they were written

out of pain

and they will always stay dear.

In my poems,

I talked about love with doubt.

THE BLACK WIDOW by Charles Bennett

Never seeing it,

never tasting its sweetness in my mouth.

Yearning to feel kept my poems real.

Being disappointed so many times

helped turn my heart as cold as steel.

And that's when I wrote.

When I gave up all hope.

Writing down my feelings

to help me cope.

But with you,

I just can't write poems that are blue.

I just want to write the words

over & over, I love you.

What am I going to do?

It was better when I miss it.

It was better when I kept it a secret.

My poetry told the truth, so that's why I hid it.

But I come to you, and I want to share.

I come to you, because I care.

THE BLACK WIDOW by Charles Bennett

I come to you, but now

you are no longer here.

I finally found the right words to write.

My mighty pen strikes this paper

as if it was fragile skin with a knife.

Now I am revealed,

see my life.

You open me,

you expose my sensitivity.

Put it like this,

you inspire me to write so heavenly.

I used to write about lost love.

Dreaming about love.

But never once thinking.

What if I fell in love?

Until, I met you.

Joshua!

Now that your gone.

What am I going to do?

(lights black out)

THE BLACK WIDOW by Charles Bennett

ACT 9
SCENE 1

(ZANE and the PROPERTY MANAGER sitting at a table as in Act One.)

PROPERTY MANAGER:

Man! What a sad story.

ZANE:

Yeah I know, but some love stories just don't have a happy ending.

PROPERTY MANAGER:

So she was sorry for what she did and was still in love with him?

ZANE:

Yeah! If he was only patient, he would've found out the truth. That Rose didn't hate him and she had the cure. She was pressured by Lily to go along with the voodoo spell.

PROPERTY MANAGER:

Since Joshua's business partner Luciano sold you this place, what is his next move?

ZANE:

A few months after Joshua died, he closed the bar down and flew out to Berkeley California. He wanted to spend more time with his family. Since then, he has been going back and forth to Cali. One of Cynthia's cousins just got out of prison for selling weed, and he just got into that program in Oakland to start a marijuana dispensary. Luciano saw money and decided to sell the bar.

PROPERTY MANAGER:

Did he and his ex-wife finally get back together?

ZANE:

Well at least not yet, but he said he just wanted to be close to his kids anyways.

PROPERTY MANAGER:

What happened to Rose?

ZANE:

She ended up getting a teaching job in Akron at Lebron James' "I Promise School." She's just having a hard time finding a good reasonable daycare for her son Heru. I gave her the five thousand I owed Joshua, but the cost of daycare is a bitch. That will only last her about four or five months.

PROPERTY MANAGER:

She had a baby?

ZANE:

Yeah, she had gotten pregnant by Joshua before he passed away. Isn't that crazy. Knowing how much he cared about family.

PROPERTY MANAGER:

What about the Rose's cousin Lily. What ever happened to her?

ZANE:

After Joshua's death, Lily thought of herself as a voodoo queen.
Using her spells to get money, cars, she was getting out of control.
Until the shit caught up with her, Lily decided she wasn't going to
pay for weed anymore. So she put a spell on her weed man and he has
been stalking her ass ever since. Her and her damn spells. Karma is a
bitch.

PROPERTY MANAGER:

Well the one thing positive that came out of Lily's spells was given
somebody a second chance at life.

ZANE:

What are you talking about?

PROPERTY MANAGER:

Remember when you said Lily and Rose grandmother told them the
terms of the spell. That his soul will never find any rest. Well now it
all make sense.

ZANE:

What on earth are you talking about?

PROPERTY MANAGER:

Put it to you like this. If I was going to give somebody a nickname, it
would have to be a name from a classical movie. See if you can guess
this one. It's this legendary hero who wears all black and kicks major
ass. Well he gets badly injured and can't protect the people until he

heals. So this hero gets his twin brother to pretend he is him and keep the legend going.

ZANE:

Wait a damn minute.

PROPERTY MANAGER:

(continues) The only thing is his twin brother is a homosexual and he doesn't want to wear all black like his brother. Instead of fighting with a sword, he rather use a whip. You know what movie I'm talking about Zane?

ZANE:

Zorro the Gay Blade, holy shit.

PROPERTY MANAGER:

I gave you that nickname after you told me the story of you and Angela fighting with knives. I said instead of you grabbing that butcher knife, you probably would've been better off using a whip. That's when I gave you the nickname Zorro.

ZANE:

(Shocked and confused: the PROPERTY MANAGER has dreadlocks and a full beard unlike JOSHUA)

I saw you die. How the hell are you still alive?

THE BLACK WIDOW by Charles Bennett

PROPERTY MANAGER:

Z, I couldn't remember shit. Talking to you now help me fill in all the gaps of who I was and what had happened. I remember waking up to the sound of thunder and lighting. The men at the cemetery must have never finished putting the dirt on my casket because I was able to climb out. I just remember walking and listening to the thunder erupting over and over again. The lighting was illuminating the night sky as I continued to walk and when the storm was finally over. I was standing in front of my Grandmother's house. I could remember where I hid the spare key. I kept getting flashes of my memories like this place, I still had a set of keys so I kept coming back. Trying and searching to find anything about my past but most importantly to find Rose.

ZANE:

(amazed) Joshua!

(ZANE rushes over to hug him)

So I guess true love never dies huh!

PROPERTY MANAGER:

If you got a voodoo spell on you, I guess not.

ZANE:

I'm just glad yo' ass ain't a zombie! (both laughing)

PROPERTY MANAGER:

I guess I got a letter "Z" for my nickname now. Man I missed yo' ass, but Zane I gotta go!

THE BLACK WIDOW by Charles Bennett

ZANE:

Where the hell are you going?

PROPERTY MANAGER:

Akron! I'm still alive, ain't I!

(ZANE nods in agreement)

Well then, I gotta go take care of my family.

(PROPERTY MANAGER turns to walk away)

ZANE:

Wait Josh before you go.

(reaches into his pocket and gives JOSHUA five hundred dollar bills)

Get Rose and your son Heru something nice.

(they hug each other again and JOSHUA leaves)

(ZANE walks toward the door and turns off all the lights except for the stage. Turns back to the stage.)

Go to your family Josh. In the words of the late Nipsey Hussle, "The marathon continues."

(lights black out)

-- END

THE BLACK WIDOW by Charles Bennett

Charles Bennett is a single parent living in Cleveland, Ohio with his son, Brandon. He is a college graduate in his forties now working in a field that he did not go to school for... which is the story of many college graduates. He attended Alabama State University, where he studied theatre under the leadership of Dr. Tommie Stewart, John Bagley and Ramona Broomer. He is grateful to them for encouraging his creative ambitions. *The Black Widow* incorporates Bennett's poetry into the drama. This is his first self-published book, and he hopes that the readers will value the overall message in this play.